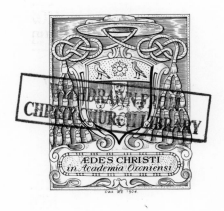

ÆDES CHRISTI
in Academia Oxoniensi

The Faber Book of Ballads

The
Faber Book of
Ballads

EDITED BY
MATTHEW HODGART

FABER & FABER
24 Russell Square
London

First published in mcmlxv
by Faber and Faber Limited
24 Russell Square London W.C.1
Printed in Great Britain by
R. MacLehose and Company Limited
The University Press Glasgow
All rights reserved

Contents

CONTENTS

8

CONTENTS

CONTENTS

Introduction

A ballad is a song that comments on life by telling a story in a
popular style. That is, to say the least, a broad definition, but it
is perhaps the narrowest that will cover all the verse in this
selection. It would, of course, cover a good deal more, such as
the love-lyrics of folk-song, various kinds of ribaldry, even
nursery-rhymes, since almost all of these tell some kind of story,
as well as offering a comment. But I have preferred to choose,
from the more clearly narrative band of the spectrum of folk-
song and popular verse, such things as have generally passed
for ballads in common usage. These are of two main kinds, which
we may call Country and Town, so apparently antipathetic that
they are seldom found together in one anthology. The most
famous of the Country ballads are the traditional Anglo-
Scottish songs assembled by F. J. Child in his great edition;
whereas the Town ballads are chiefly represented by the 'broadsides'. Despite great differences of style, outlook and often of
poetic merit, the two kinds are alike in one respect; they do not
belong to the Great Tradition of our civilization, but they
speak for 'the people'.

The Great Tradition is, I take it, the sum of the skills and
crafts of the most creative and educated members of a civilization: it includes the language of science, religion, law and
learning, as well as 'serious' literature. In the English-speaking
world it means, among other things, the succession of great
writers from Chaucer onwards, and a literature based at first on
the English Court and today mainly on the capital cities and
universities of Britain, the Commonwealth and North America.
But this Great Tradition has never made up the whole of our
civilization, and although it has set the ultimate standards in
life and art it has never been whole-heartedly accepted by or
even available to many members of the community. Perhaps the

11

last moment in history when the best in art and literature belonged to the whole people was at the height of classical Athens; but even then the 'people', although it included town and country, rich and poor, did not include slaves—or women. Certainly since then every civilization has also possessed its 'little traditions', which form much of the culture of backward areas or depressed classes; of peasant or small-farmer communities, whose education and even literacy are at a low level, and the poorer town-dwellers, 'on the wrong side of the tracks'. The sum of these little traditions is called 'folk-lore', a term that is usually applied to the inherited crafts, beliefs, dances, stories and songs of country-people, but can quite legitimately be used of urban arts, like the striking children's games collected by Norman Douglas in London. It is better to use the plural form, 'traditions', since in the nature of things folk-lore cannot be unified: it varies with region and occupation; many strands make up a rich and disorderly pattern, as in the ballads of this book. The Great Tradition is based on Standard English, the little traditions in the various dialects (hence the difficulty many readers will find with the language of the ballads). Like the dialects, the little traditions are local, often highly conservative and archaic, preserving the past long after it has disappeared from the centre of civilization: traces of medieval ways of life and pre-Christian beliefs are found in even quite late versions of some ballads. These traditions are by-products—and at their best splendid by-products—of a poverty-stricken economy and wretched communications, but they are never quite independent of the Great Tradition. Ideas and themes, art-forms and conventions, spread, however slowly, from the creative centre to the outlying regions, where they may be preserved throughout the centuries like ants in amber. Conversely, the educated sharers of the Great Tradition have always been attracted by folklore. We are all Rousseauists or Wordsworthians to the degree that we are discontented with the artificiality of our culture, and many see the unsophisti-

cated charms of folk-lore as analogous to the happiness of a
vanished childhood. There is always some cult of the 'natural'
or the 'primitive' in fashion among the learned, some wish to
equate goodness in life or art with ancient times or simple
people. So most of the good English-speaking poets have
admired ballads, lyrical, satirical or plain bawdy, and have
taken something from them into their art; and, as we shall see,
many have written them too.

Among the most ancient of our little traditions is the Country
ballad, which has a continuous history from the fifteenth
century to the present. It is represented by the 'Traditional'
ballads of section I of this book. This is a form, which has taken
up many kinds of stories—supernatural, realistic, tragic and
comic—and transformed them by its special style. The form is
really two allied forms; of which the first is the couplet with a
refrain in alternate lines,

> She sat down below a thorn,
> *Fine flowers in the valley,*
> And there she has her sweet babe born,
> *And the green leaves they grow rarely,*

which descends from a singing-dance of the Middle Ages, better
represented in the Danish and Faroese ballads. The second is
the usual quatrain in Common Measure (4–3–4–3), which was
used by the minstrels for longer narratives, like *Chevy Chase.*
Both belonged originally to aristocratic entertainment, and
passed by degrees to the people. The connexion with the dance
was lost in Britain but that with song has always remained. In
fact, the ballads are essentially music and come to life fully
only when they leave the printed page; and it is a pity that
there is no room in this selection for their tunes, many of them
extremely beautiful. The musical and metrical form helped to
produce their uniquely dramatic style: the story is told in sharp
flashes, with a distinct scene or a separate passage of dialogue
in each stanza. The singer dramatizes the action in the most

emphatic manner he knows, omitting everything that is unnecessary to a swift climax.

After the ballads' dramatic quality, the next most striking feature of their style is the 'commonplace' or 'formula'.* It is 'the gold so red' that adorns the heroine, 'the wan water' that the messenger must cross, and he often crosses it in a complete two-line, seven-stress formula: 'And when he came to the wan water, He bent his bow and swam'. Everyone will have noticed that ballads are built up with recurrent themes: the plants that grow from the lovers' graves and twine together, the lady standing on the castle wall, the exchanging of angry words, the taking of vows of austerity. A formula is a theme expressed in identical or almost identical words and metre; thus in seven ballads we find a variant of the phrase 'When bells were rung and mass was sung, And all men bound for bed'. That is put in, not to make any special point about religion, but simply to express the idea that time passed and night came, and to express it in a time-honoured way. It is analogous to the formula used in Homeric epic (such as the rosy-fingered dawn, the wine-dark sea, or Achilles fleet of foot) and in the modern Yugoslavian epic, which has been studied so fruitfully by Milman Parry and A. B. Lord.† The ballad formula, like the Homeric, has almost certainly its origin in oral tradition. The singers could not read, and although they had wonderful memories, they did not aim at reproducing a text exactly, but simply at telling the old stories in the old way. When they came to a point in the story that called for a curse or a lover's night visit, they drew without hesitation from the wide repertoire of stock phrases that they all knew: 'O wae betide you, ill woman . . .' or 'Open and let me in'. No two versions of a ballad are ever exactly alike; and every singer is both a transmitter of tradition and an original composer. But whereas literary poets compose with individual

* See James H. Jones, 'Commonplace and Memorisation in the Oral Tradition of the English and Scottish Popular Ballads', *Journal of American Folklore* (1961).
† *The Singer of Tales*, 1960.

words which they shape into new phrases, oral poets compose with complete themes and formulae, because they know of no other way. Even when an unusually creative singer produced a new ballad on contemporary events, he would use the traditional formulae, perhaps centuries old, for his new story; and this above all gives the traditional ballads their family likeness. It is not suggested that every ballad came to birth in this way—indeed, there are many that cannot have done so—but the conditions of oral composition and oral transmission set their stamp on every 'Child' ballad.

The old ballads are alike in other ways. They prefer tragic stories, which are told laconically and impersonally, yet with a strong feeling for the glory and impermanence of human life. What the singers admire is a heroic way of life, in which loyalty to kinsmen and to lovers are the supreme values, even when they are in hopeless conflict. It is a folk version of the medieval chivalric code and of Courtly Love. Yet in some ways the ballads go back even beyond the Middle Ages, to the ancient Germanic epic tradition (as in 'Earl Brand') and to Celtic legend and myth. The Scottish ballads, in particular, show a rich harvest of beliefs in magic, ghosts, witches and fairies which must have grown from pre-Christian religion; whereas Christian mythology and ethics touched them only a little. This type of ballad is not only the most archaic but shows the closest kinship, in stories, motifs, outlook and even formulae, with European balladry and folklore.

The ballads in the next section, 'Robin Hood and Border', are by no means so archaic although some have earlier texts. They descend from the medieval minstrel's art; they are less formulaic and probably more dependent on written versions from the beginning. 'Chevy Chase' is a minstrel's celebration of the heroic and more or less historical deeds of the noble houses of Percy and Douglas. The Robin Hood ballads show how minstrelsy has been transferred from aristocratic to yeoman patronage. Who Robin Hood was is still a vexed question, but

there is less doubt about what the ballads express: rebellious-
ness towards feudalism and the Establishment, the kind of
primitive revolt which prefers to politics the glorification of the
brigand hero. Robin Hood, though technically a criminal and
the enemy of sheriff and bishop, is the friend of the poor. Songs
about him may date from the Peasants' Revolt of the late fourteenth century; certainly about that time Langland's Sloth
knew 'rhymes of Robin Hood and Ranulf Earl of Chester'. (It
has been suggested, incidentally, that since there was a story
about poisoning associated with this Ranulf he may be the
original of 'Lord Randal my son'.) The true 'Border' ballads are
also celebrations of outlawry: they concern the exploits, often
in cattle-thieving, of the anarchic and barely tamed Lowland
clans: they are mostly of the sixteenth century, and, despite the
name, their setting is Aberdeenshire as much as South Scotland. The Robin Hood and Border ballads are local in origin
and do not belong to international folklore; but like the
Spanish ballads and the Yugoslavian epics they breathe the
air of 'frontier', mountain or forest, where crime and the heroic
life are never far apart.

In the more settled conditions of eighteenth-century Scotland
something new happened which changed the history and literary prestige of balladry. There seems to have been a number of
people who possessed both great literary talent and an intuitive
understanding of the ballad tradition; and who were thus able
to create not only the finest versions in existence of certain old
ballads, but also splendid new ones that are completely in the
traditional style. Sir Walter Scott is the best-known example:
he collected assiduously, polished up versions which he thought
too crude, and wrote at least one complete ballad, 'Kinmont
Willie', in the Border style. Before Scott there was Robert
Burns, whose work as editor, improver, and original composer
of folksongs can hardly be distinguished today, so faithfully did
he capture the spirit and style of folksong. Unfortunately
Burns was not greatly interested in ballads, since he preferred

bawdy and love lyrics; but his hand can be seen in some stanzas of the version of 'Tam Lin' which he sent to the *Scots Musical Museum*. Burns, even to a greater degree than Scott, illustrates the peculiar nature of this community in which educated men had immediate access to the rich treasures of folkloric tradition. There must have been others before him. It has long been suspected that the superlative versions of 'Edward' and 'Lord Thomas' sent to Bishop Percy for his *Reliques* (1765) show signs of literary reshaping; and recently Mr B. H. Bronson has given good reasons for supposing that other versions and ballads had a largely or purely literary origin in the eighteenth century. The classic case is the great text of 'Sir Patrick Spens' printed by Percy, which may be as complete a fabrication as the notorious 'Hardicanute'. This makes no difference whatsoever to the standing of 'Sir Patrick Spens'; in style and dramatic quality it is outstanding among the ballads of the world, and it is so close to tradition that it was taken up by the folk-singers and acquired other versions. Again, 'The Twa Corbies' may be a very late and individual version of the highly archaic and folkloric 'Three Ravens'. Although I have printed these two together under 'Traditional' as an interesting comparison of styles, I have placed the other eighteenth-century Scots classics in a separate section.

In the next section there are a few lyrical songs from the boundary-line of balladry, some of them not given recognition by Child. They are laments, songs of separation and a few religious ballads. In some the speaker or singer must be a woman; it is a reasonably safe generalisation that the heroic ballad is a masculine art, the pathetic folk-lyric largely a feminine one. 'The Unquiet Grave' and 'Still Growing' are outstanding for the purity of their sorrow, and for their variety of piercingly beautiful tunes. To these there could be added hundreds of other folksongs, which have some claim to be called ballads; but what I have printed in the first four sections and described so far should show some of the range of the traditional ballad. But there are still many other things which can legitimately be called ballads, and this brings up the curious problems of the name.

How the ballads came to be called by their name makes a curious story, which has only recently been worked out by Mr A. B. Friedman.* The word originally came from Latin *ballare*, to dance, and the Provençal form *ballada* was used in the earlier Middle Ages to describe various dance-songs and verse-forms derived from them, but *not* apparently for the narrative poems we now call ballads. From this were derived the Italian *ballata*, a lyric with an elaborately rhymed stanza, and the French *ballade*, which in the fourteenth and fifteenth centuries meant one particular and complex verse-form, with rhymes a b a b b c b C, the last line being a refrain. The best-known example is Villon's 'Ballade des dames du temps jadis', with its refrain 'Mais où sont les neiges d'antan?' The word was taken over into English, and the verse-form much imitated, if not always strictly, in English verse of the fifteenth century; but for some reason it was used mainly for political and social verse, satires and complaints of topical interest. When cheap printing began in England in the early sixteenth century, many 'ballads' of this kind were written and issued as broadsides, because they were good propaganda; as for example this fragment of an anti-Papist ballad:

> They had false prophets which brought
>   thinges to passe
> Cleane contrary to ther owne expectacion;
> Ther hope was for helpe in ther popishe masse,
> They wolde nedes have hanged up a reservacion.
> The vicare of pon wdstoke with   [Woodstock
>   his congeracion
> Commanded them to sticke to their Idolatry

* A. B. Friedman, *The Ballad Revival*, 1961

> They had much provision and grete preparacion
> [REFRAIN]   Yet God hath gyven our kynge the victorye.*

The name then spread to other broadside verse of a topical nature, which was not written in the ballade or near-ballade form. John Skelton's *A Ballade of the Scottyshe Kynge* (above, p. 161) is thought to be the oldest printed broadside ballad, written and issued soon after the Battle of Flodden in 1513; and it is in rough doggerel rhyming couplets. Broadside ballads throughout their history have been written in several kinds of metre, but from the middle of the sixteenth century commonly in the normal quatrain of folk-song, because the broadsides were meant to be sung to well-known tunes. Now, since, the country narrative songs were mostly in this quatrain form, and since some of them were printed as broadsides, they too became known as ballads, and finally all but usurped the name.

A broadside is a small sheet of paper, roughly printed on one side, and sold cheaply in the market-place or fair by hawkers. All kinds of things were printed on broadsides, but from the sixteenth century the 'broadside ballad' took on a characteristic form: a new song to an old tune, which gave a commentary on the affairs of the day. The tune is often indicated on the top of the sheet, and the seller would sing it to the crowd to advertise his wares. It did many of the things now divided between the newspapers, television and the topical revue. Politics, or 'affairs of state' were a favourite topic, from Skelton onwards; but the Town Ballad also described marvellous events, told bawdy stories, and voiced complaints against social abuses; sang, in fact, everything likely to interest the urban public. That public included domestic servants, pre-industrial workers and apprentices and the half-literate 'mob' of London, whose turbulence and licentiousness were so often noted by foreign travellers in the eighteenth century. The form lends itself easily to satire, and was felt to have political influence;

* *The Common Muse,* ed. V. de Sola Pinto and A. E. Rodway, p. 34.

perhaps for this reason, as well as for its ungodliness, ballad singing was prohibited during the Commonwealth under severe penalties, though broadsides went on being printed. Although most broadside ballads were written by obscure hacks, several famous writers have used the form to spread their views to the widest possible public. Swift's 'Drapier' ballads were an important part of his successful campaign against the English Government on the issue of 'Wood's Halfpence'; and other examples of broadside satire from Marvell to Dickens can be found in this selection. To all English writers from Shakespeare up to Wordsworth, the word 'ballad' meant a broadside: something that belonged to the people and especially to Londoners, 'low' or 'vulgar' if you liked, but an expression of free speech and democratic protest.

The brutality of the old town life is reflected in a favourite type of broadside, the 'criminal's last goodnight'.* This goes back to the beheading of the Earl of Essex and Sir Walter Raleigh, but reached its climax in the eighteenth-century hangings at Tyburn. This was the golden age of the criminal hero, especially the highwayman: 'The youth in his cart hath the air of a Lord, And we say, There dies an Adonis', as *The Beggar's Opera* has it. John Gay's great work, the apotheosis of popular song, took its origin from a broadside Gay wrote about the arch-villain Jonathan Wild, satirically comparing statesmen with criminals. The theme of execution continues through 'The Night before Larry was Stretched' up to Kipling's 'Danny Deever'; and combined with the equally traditional theme of social protest, it reappears in Euan MacColl's 'Go Down, You Murderers' and the recent anti-Apartheid song 'Hanging on a Tree'. The broadside remains faithful to its origins.

During the nineteenth century broadsides continued to be written and sold in vast numbers, but the literary quality of the

---

* There is an excellent study of the genre by A. B. Friedman in his *Viking Book of Folk Ballads*.

London popular Muse declined. It was otherwise in Ireland, where the political situation and the national talent for song kept the broadside alive from the Rising of 1798 to the Troubles of the 1920's. The Dublin street-ballads are a microcosm of Dublin life, treating the great subjects of sport, drink, love and nationalism with verbal fluency and melodic delicacy. Because so many of them lie on the edge of burlesque, they have never been taken seriously enough in England, but they affected almost every Irish writer. James Joyce, who describes the nasal whine of the singers of 'Come-all-you's', quotes from street-ballads throughout his work, and most of all in *Finnegans Wake*, itself based on a comic song. In the second chapter of that fantastic work, the hero is attacked by the hostile populace in a ballad which parodies the genre with dreamlike extravagance.

The Irish, transported to Van Diemen's Land for politics or poaching, took the ballad with them. Hence Australian balladry is closer to the broadside than to the Country tradition: there is a good deal of it, but perhaps of greater historical than literary interest. The basis of North American balladry, on the other hand, is the traditional 'Child' ballad. Dozens of the old Country songs were brought over by English and Scottish settlers between the seventeenth and nineteenth centuries, and they survived to a surprising degree in isolated communities of the Appalachians, Maine and other forest or mountain areas, where literacy was low and there was little competition from other forms of art. The American versions of 'Child' ballads printed here show how faithfully ancient traits were preserved by these highlanders, and the same is true of their beautiful modal melodies. I have put 'Barbara Allen' among the American songs, although it is in Child, since in the U.S.A. it was so widespread and helped to set the style of the native balladry of the plains and cities. The plains ballad also had its ancestry in the broadside, but had a vigorous life of its own in the nineteenth century. It has been shown, for example, how 'The Cowboy's Lament', or 'The Streets of Laredo', derives from an eighteenth-century Irish song called 'The Unfortunate Rake', through English broadsides. But from such beginnings the cowboys, lumberjacks and railway workers developed their various songs to express their way of life, as the Frontier moved westwards. In the cities, the broadside-type of song about politics and crime found an encouraging milieu, and in the late nineteenth and early twentieth century came to surpass its English equivalent. But at this point the American ballad shades off into the vast field of work-song, gospel song, blues and jazz, where this anthology can no longer pursue it. I am aware that I have also had to leave out many aspects of British folk-song which lie on the fringe of balladry—sea-shanties, miners' songs, bothy ballads and so on. Thanks to the present revival of folk-singing these are in no danger of being neglected.

In the last few years folk-song of every kind has become available, through books, gramophone records and radio programmes, to everyone. Collectors with tape-recorders have perhaps swept up the last crumbs of the Country tradition remaining in Britain and America, and by now much more has been filed away in the archives than can ever be published. Meanwhile the ballad has taken on new life among CND marchers in Britain and Freedom Riders in America, who are themselves but part of a greater army of guitar-players; and folk-song has already precedence over jazz in the hearts of most university students. Paradoxically, song from the old popular traditions has even affected 'pop' music; to say more would be to step into the quicksands of sociology. What is certain is that the ballad is history and it lives.

I

Traditional

TRADITIONAL

Riddles Wisely Expounded

There was a knicht riding frae the east,
  Sing the Cather banks, the bonnie brume
Wha had been wooing at monie a place.
  And ye may beguile a young thing sune.

He came unto a widow's door.
And speird whare her three dochters were.

The auldest ane's to the washing gane,
The second's to a baking gane.

The youngest ane's to a wedding gane,
And it will be nicht or she be hame.

He sat him doun upon a stane,
Till thir three lasses came tripping hame.

The auldest ane's to the bed making,
And the second ane's to the sheet spreading.

The youngest ane was bauld and bricht,
And she was to lye wi' this unco knicht.

'Gin ye will answer me questions ten,
This morn ye sall be made my ain.

'O what is heigher nor the tree?
And what is deeper nor the sea?

'Or what is heavier nor the lead?
And what is better nor the breid?

'O what is whiter nor the milk?
Or what is safter nor the silk?

'Or what is sharper nor a thorn?
Or what is louder nor a horn?

'Or what is greener nor the grass?
Or what is waur nor a woman was?'

'O heaven is higher nor the tree,
And hell is deeper nor the sea.

'O sin is heavier nor the lead,
The blessing's better than the bread.

'The snaw is whiter nor the milk,
And the down is safter nor the silk.

'Hunger is sharper nor a thorn,
And shame is louder nor a horn.

'The pies are greener nor the grass,
And Clootie's waur nor a woman was.'

As sune as she the fiend did name,
He flew awa in a blazing flame.

The Elfin Knight

My plaid awa, my plaid awa,
And ore the hill and far awa,
And far awa to Norrowa,
My plaid shall not be blown awa.

TRADITIONAL

The elfin knight sits on yon hill,
  Ba, ba, lilli ba
He blaws his horn both lowd and shril.
  The wind hath blown my plaid awa

He blowes it east, he blowes it west,
He blowes it where he lyketh best.

'I wish that horn were in my kist,
Yea, and the knight in my armes two.'

She had no sooner these words said,
When that the knight came to her bed.

'Thou art over young a maid,' quoth he,
'Married with me thou il wouldst be.'

'I have a sister younger than I,
And she was married yesterday.'

'Married with me if thou wouldst be,
A courtesie thou must do to me.

'For thou must shape a sark to me,
Without any cut or heme,' quoth he.

'Thou must shape it knife-and-sheerlesse,
And also sue it needle-threadlesse.'

'If that piece of courtesie I do to thee,
Another thou must do to me.

'I have an aiker of good ley-land,
Which lyeth low by yon sea-strand.

'For thou must eare it with thy horn,
So thou must sow it with thy corn.

27

'And bigg a cart of stone and lyme,
Robin Redbreast he must trail it hame.

'Thou must barn it in a mouse-holl,
And thrash it into thy shoes' soll.

'And thou must winnow it in thy looff,
And also seek it in thy glove.

'For thou must bring it over the sea,
And thou must bring it dry home to me.

'When thou has gotten thy turns well done,
Then come to me and get thy sark then.'

'I'l not quit my plaid for my life;
It haps my seven bairns and my wife.'
The wind shall not blow my plaid awa

'My maidenhead I'l then keep still,
Let the elphin knight do what he will.'
The wind's not blown my plaid awa

Lady Isabel and the Elf-Knight

Fair lady Isabel sits in her bower sewing,
Aye as the gowans grow gay
There she heard an elf-knight blawing his horn.
The first morning in May.

'If I had yon horn that I hear blawing,
And yon elf-knight to sleep in my bosom.'

This maiden had scarcely these words spoken,
Till in at her window the elf-knight has luppen.

'It's a very strange matter, fair maiden,' said he,
'I canna blaw my horn but ye call on me.

'But will ye go to yon greenwood side?
If ye canna gang, I will cause you to ride.'

He leapt on a horse, and she on another,
And they rode on to the greenwood together.

'Light down, light down, lady Isabel,' said he,
'We are come to the place where ye are to die.'

'Hae mercy, hae mercy, kind sir, on me,
Till ance my dear father and mother I see.'

'Seven king's-daughters here hae I slain,
And ye shall be the eight o them.'

'O sit down a while, lay your head on my knee,
That we may hae some rest before that I die.'

She stroakd him sae fast, the nearer he did creep,
Wi' a sma charm she lull'd him fast asleep.

Wi' his ain sword-belt sae fast as she ban him,
Wi' his ain dag-durk sae sair as she dang him.

'If seven king's-daughters here ye hae slain,
Lye ye here, a husband to them a'.'

Earl Brand
(*The Douglas Tragedy*)

'Rise up, rise up, my seven brave sons,
    And dress in your armour so bright;
Earl Douglas will hae Lady Margaret awa
    Before that it be light.

TRADITIONAL

'Arise, arise, my seven brave sons,
   And dress in your armour so bright;
It shall never be said that a daughter of mine
   Shall go with an earl or a knight.'

'Oh will ye stand, fair Margaret,' he says,
   'And hold my milk-white steed,
Till I fight your father and seven brethren,
   In yonder pleasant mead?'

She stood and held his milk-white steed,
   She stood trembling with fear,
Until she saw her seven brethren fall,
   And her father that loved her dear.

'Hold your hand, Earl Douglas,' she says,
   'Your strokes are wonderous sair;
I may get sweethearts again enew,
   But a father I'll ne'er get mair.'

She took out a handkerchief,
   Was made o' the cambrick fine,
And aye she wiped her father's bloody wounds,
   And the blood sprung up like wine.

'Will ye go, fair Margaret?' he said,
   'Will ye now go, or bide?'
'Yes, I'll go, sweet William,' she said,
   'For ye've left me never a guide.

'If I were to go to my mother's house,
   A welcome guest I would be;
But for the bloody deed that's done this day,
   I'll rather go with thee.'

He lifted her on a milk-white steed
   And himself on a dapple gray;

They drew their hats out over their face,
  And they both went weeping away.

They rode, they rode, and they better rode,
  Till they came to yon water wan;
They lighted down to gie their horse a drink
  Out of the running stream.

'I am afraid, Earl Douglas,' she said,
  'I am afraid ye are slain;
I think I see your bonny heart's blood
  Running down the water wan.'

'Oh no, oh no, fair Margaret,' he said,
  'Oh no, I am not slain;
It is but the scad of my scarlet cloak
  Runs down the water wan.'

He mounted her on a milk-white steed
  And himself on a dapple gray,
And they have reached Earl Douglas' gates
  Before the break of day.

'O rise, dear mother, and make my bed,
  And make it braid and wide,
And lay me down to take my rest,
  And at my back my bride.'

She has risen and made his bed,
  She made it braid and wide;
She laid him down to take his rest,
  And at his back his bride.

Lord William died ere it was day,
  Lady Margaret on the morrow;
Lord William died through loss of blood and wounds,
  Lady Margaret died with sorrow.

The one was buried in Mary's kirk,
   The other in Mary's quire;
The one sprung up a bonny bush,
   And the other a bonny brier.

These twa grew, and these twa threw,
   Till they came to the top,
And when they could na farther gae,
   They coost the lovers' knot.

The Twa Sisters

There was twa sisters in a bow'r,
   Edinburgh, Edinburgh
There was twa sisters in a bow'r,
   Stirling for ay
There was twa sisters in a bow'r,
There came a knight to be their wooer.
   Bonny Saint Johnston stands upon Tay.

He courted the eldest wi' glove and ring,
But he lov'd the youngest above a' thing.

He courted the eldest wi' brotch an knife,
But lov'd the youngest as his life.

The eldest she was vexed sair,
An' much envi'd her sister fair.

Into her bow'r she could not rest,
Wi' grief an' spite she almos' brast.

Upon a morning fair an' clear,
She cried upon her sister dear:

TRADITIONAL

'O sister, come to yon sea stran',
An' see our father's ships come to lan'.'

She's ta'en her by the milk-white han',
An' led her down to yon sea stran'.

The younges' stood upon a stane,
The eldest came an' threw her in.

She tooke her by the middle sma',
An' dashed her bonny back to the jaw.

'O sister, sister, tak' my han',
An I'se mack you heir to a' my lan'.

'O sister, sister, tak' my middle,
An' ye's get my goud and my gouden girdle.

'O sister, sister, save my life,
An' I swear I'se never be nae man's wife.'

'Foul fa' the han' that I should tacke,
It twin'd me an my wardles make.

'Your cherry cheeks an' yallow hair
Gars me gae maiden for evermair.'

Sometimes she sank, an' sometimes she swam,
Till she came down yon bonny mill-dam.

O out it came the miller's son,
An' saw the fair maid swimmin' in.

'O father, father, draw your dam,
Here's either a mermaid or a swan.'

The miller quickly drew the dam,
An' there he found a drown'd woman.

You cou'dna see her yallow hair
For gold and pearle that were so rare.

You cou'dna see her middle sma'
For gouden girdle that was sae braw.

You cou'dna see her fingers white,
For gouden rings that was sae gryte.

An' by there came a harper fine,
That harped to the king at dine.

When he did look that lady upon,
He sigh'd and made a heavy moan.

He's ta'en three locks o her yallow hair,
An' wi' them strung his harp sae fair.

The first tune he did play and sing,
Was, 'Farewell to my father the king.'

The nextin tune that he play'd syne,
Was, 'Farewell to my mother the queen.'

The lasten tune that he play'd then,
Was, 'Wae to my sister, fair Ellen.'

Lord Randal

'O where ha you been, Lord Randal, my son?
And where ha you been, my handsome young man?'
'I ha been at the greenwood; mother, mak my bed soon,
For I'm wearied wi hunting, and fain wad lie down.'

'An wha met ye there, Lord Randal, my son?
An wha met you there, my handsome young man?'
'O I met wi my true-love; mother, mak my bed soon,
For I'm wearied wi hunting, and fain wad lie down.'

'And what did she give you, Lord Randal, my son?
And what did she give you, my handsome young man?'
'Eels fried in a pan; mother, mak my bed soon,
For I'm wearied wi huntin, and fain wad lie down.'

'An wha gat your leavins, Lord Randal, my son?
And wha gat your leavins, my handsome young man?'
'My hawks and my hounds; mother, mak my bed soon,
For I'm wearied wi huntin, and fain wad lie down.'

'And what becam of them, Lord Randal, my son?
And what becam of them, my handsome young man?'
'They stretched their legs out and died; mother, mak my bed
   soon,
For I'm wearied wi huntin, and fain wad lie down.'

'O I fear you are poisoned, Lord Randal, my son!
I fear you are poisoned, my handsome young man!'
'O yes, I am poisoned; mother, mak my bed soon,
For I'm sick at the heart, and I fain wad lie down.'

'What d'ye leave to your mother, Lord Randal, my son?
What d'ye leave to your mother, my handsome young man?'
'Four and twenty milk kye; mother, mak my bed soon,
For I'm sick at the heart, and I fain wad lie down.'

'What d'ye leave to your sister, Lord Randal, my son?
What d'ye leave to your sister, my handsome young man?'
'My gold and my silver; mother, mak my bed soon,
For I'm sick at the heart, an I fain wad lie down.'

'What d'ye leave to your brother, Lord Randal, my son?
What d'ye leave to your brother, my handsome young man?'
'My houses and my lands; mother, mak my bed soon,
For I'm sick at the heart, and I fain wad lie down.'

'What d'ye leave to your true-love, Lord Randal, my son?
What d'ye leave to your true-love, my handsome young man?'
'I leave her hell and fire; mother, mak my bed soon,
For I'm sick at the heart, and I fain wad lie down.'

The Cruel Mother

She sat down below a thorn,
 Fine flowers in the valley
And there she has her sweet babe born.
 And the green leaves they grow rarely

'Smile na sae sweet, my bonie babe,
And ye smile sae sweet, ye'll smile me dead.'

She's taen out her little pen-knife,
And twinnd the sweet babe o its life.

She's howket a grave by the light o the moon,
And there she's buried her sweet babe in.

As she was going to the church,
She saw a sweet babe in the porch.

'O sweet babe, and thou were mine,
I wad cleed thee in the silk so fine.'

'O mother dear, when I was thine,
You did na prove to me sae kind.'

The Three Ravens

There were three ravens sat on a tree,
    Downe a downe, hay down, hay downe
There were three ravens sat on a tree,
    With a downe
There were three ravens sat on a tree,
They were as black as they might be,
    With a downe derrie, derrie, derrie, downe, downe.

The one of them said to his mate,
'Where shall we our breakfast take?'

'Down in yonder greene field,
There lies a knight slain under his shield.

'His hounds they lie down at his feete,
So well they can their master keepe.

'His haukes they flie so eagerly,
There's no fowle dare him come nie.'

Downe there comes a fallow doe,
As great with yong as she might goe.

She lift up his bloudy hed,
And kist his wounds that were so red.

She got him up upon her backe,
And carried him to earthen lake.

She buried him before the prime,
She was dead herselfe ere even-song time.

God send every gentleman
Such haukes, such hounds, and such a leman.

The Twa Corbies

As I was walking all alane,
  I heard twa corbies making a mane;
The tane unto the t'other say,
  'Where sall we gang and dine to-day?'

'In behint yon auld fail dyke,
  I wot there lies a new-slain knight;
And naebody kens that he lies there,
  But his hawk, his hound, and his lady fair.

His hound is to the hunting gane,
  His hawk, to fetch the wild-fowl hame,
His lady's ta'en another mate,
  So we may mak our dinner sweet.

Ye'll sit on his white hause-bane,
  And I'll pike out his bonny blue een.
Wi' ae lock o' his gowden hair,
  We'll theek our nest when it grows bare.

'Mony a one for him makes mane,
  But nane sall ken whare he is gane;
O'er his white banes, when they are bare,
  The wind sall blaw for evermair.'

Corpus Christi

Lully, lulley, lully, lulley,
The faucon hath borne my mak away.

He bare hym up, he bare hym down,
He bare hym into an orchard brown.

38

TRADITIONAL

In that orchard there was a hall,
That was hanged with purple and pall.

And in that hall there was a bede,
Hit was hanged with gold so rede.

And in that bed ther lythe a knyght,
His wounde bledyng day and nyght.

By that bedes side ther kneleth a may,
And she wepeth both night and day.

And by that beddes side ther stondeth a ston,
Corpus Christi wretyn theron.

Clerk Colvill

Clerk Colvill and his lusty dame
   Were walking in the garden green;
The belt around her stately waist
   Cost Clerk Colvill of pounds fifteen.

'O promise me now, Clerk Colvill,
   Or it will cost ye muckle strife,
Ride never by the wells of Slane,
   If ye wad live and brook your life.'

'Now speak nae mair, my lusty dame,
   Now speak nae mair of that to me;
Did I neer see a fair woman,
   But I wad sin with her body?'

He's taen leave o his gay lady,
   Nought minding what his lady said,
And he's rose by the wells of Slane,
   Where washing was a bonny maid.

'Wash on, wash on, my bonny maid,
    That wash sae clean your sark of silk;'
'It's a' for you, ye gentle knight,
    My skin is whiter than the milk.'

He's taen her by the milk-white hand,
    And likewise by the grass-green sleeve,
And laid her down upon the green,
    Nor of his lady speer'd he leave.

Then loud, loud cry'd the Clerk Colvill,
    'O my head it pains me sair;'
'Then take, then take,' the maiden said,
    'And frae my sark you'll cut a gare.'

Then she's gied him a little bane-knife,
    And frae her sark he cut a share;
She's ty'd it round his whey-white face,
    But ay his head it aked mair.

Then louder cry'd the Clerk Colvill,
    'O sairer, sairer akes my head.'
'And sairer, sairer ever will,'
    The maiden crys, 'till you be dead.'

Out then he drew his shining blade,
    Thinking to stick her where she stood,
But she was vanished to a fish,
    And swam far off, a fair mermaid.

'O mother, mother, braid my hair;
    My lusty lady, make my bed;
O brother, take my sword and spear,
    For I have seen the false mermaid.'

Young Beichan
(*Lord Bateman*)

In London city was Bicham born,
  He longd strange countries for to see,
But he was ta'en by a savage Moor,
  Who handld him right cruely.

For thro' his shoulder he put a bore,
  And thro' the bore has pitten a tree,
And he's gard him draw the carts o wine,
  Where horse and oxen had wont to be.

He's casten him in a dungeon deep,
  Where he coud neither hear nor see;
He's shut him up in a prison strong,
  An he's handld him right cruely.

O this Moor he had but ae daughter,
  I wot her name was Shusy Pye;
She's doen her to the prison-house,
  And she's calld Young Bicham one word by.

'O hae ye ony land or rents,
  Or citys in your ain country,
Coud free you out of prison strong,
  An coud maintain a lady free?'

'O London city is my own,
  An other citys twa or three,
Coud loose me out o prison strong,
  An coud maintain a lady free.'

41

TRADITIONAL

O she has bribed her father's men,
  Wi' meikle goud and white money,
She's gotten the key of the prison doors,
  An she has set Young Bicham free.

She's gi'n him a loaf o good white bread,
  But an a flask o Spanish wine,
An she bad him mind on the ladie's love,
  That sae kindly freed him out o pine.

'Go set your foot on good ship-board,
  An haste you back to your ain country,
An before that seven years has an end,
  Come back again, love, and marry me.'

It was long or seven years had an end
  She longd fu sair her love to see;
She's set her foot on good ship-board,
  An turnd her back on her ain country.

She's saild up, so has she doun,
  Till she came to the other side;
She's landed at Young Bicham's gates,
  And I hop this day she sal be his bride.

'Is this Young Bicham's gates?' says she,
  'Or is that noble prince within?'
'He's up the stairs wi' his bonny bride,
  An monny a lord and lady wi him.'

'O has he taen a bonny bride,
  An has he clean forgotten me!'
An sighing said that gay lady,
  'I wish I were in my ain country!'

But she's pitten her han in her pocket,
 An gin the porter guineas three;
Says, 'Take ye that, ye proud porter,
 An bid the bridegroom speak to me.'

O whan the porter came up the stair,
 He's fa'n low down upon his knee:
'Won up, won up, ye proud porter,
 An what makes a' this courtesy?'

'O I've been porter at your gates
 This mair nor seven years an three,
But there is a lady at them now
 The like of whom I never did see.

'For on every finger she has a ring,
 An on the mid-finger she has three,
An there's as meikle goud aboon her brow
 As woud buy an earldome o lan to me.'

Then up it started Young Bicham,
 An sware so loud by Our Lady,
'It can be nane but Shusy Pye,
 That has come oer the sea to me.'

O quickly ran he down the stair,
 O' fifteen steps he has made but three;
He's tane his bonny love in his arms,
 An a wot he kissd her tenderly.

'O hae you tane a bonny bride?
 An hae you quite forsaken me?
An hae ye quite forgotten her
 That gae you life an liberty?'

She's lookit oer her left shoulder
    To hide the tears stood in her ee;
'Now fare thee well, Young Bicham,' she says,
    'I'll strive to think nae mair on thee.'

'Take back your daughter, madam,' he says,
    'An a double dowry I'll gi her wi;
For I maun marry my first true love,
    That's done and suffered so much for me.'

He's take his bonny love by the han,
    And led her to yon fountain stane;
He's changed her name frae Shusy Pye,
    An he's cald her his bonny love, Lady Jane.

Fair Annie

'It's narrow, narrow make your bed,
    And learn to lie your lane;
For I'm ga'n oer the sea, Fair Annie,
    A braw bride to bring hame.
Wi her I will get gowd and gear;
    Wi you I neer got nane.

'But wha will bake my bridal bread,
    Or brew my bridal ale?
And wha will welcome my brisk bride,
    That I bring oer the dale?'

'It's I will bake your bridal bread,
    And brew your bridal ale,
And I will welcome your brisk bride,
    That you bring oer the dale.'

'But she that welcomes my brisk bride
   Maun gang like maiden fair;
She maun lace on her robe sae jimp,
   And braid her yellow hair.'

'But how can I gang maiden-like,
   When maiden I am nane?
Have I not born seven sons to thee,
   And am with child again?'

She's taen her young son in her arms,
   Another in her hand,
And she's up to the highest tower,
   To see him come to land.

'Come up, come up, my eldest son,
   And look oer yon sea-strand,
And see your father's new-come bride,
   Before she come to land.'

'Come down, come down, my mother dear,
   Come frae the castle wa!
I fear, if langer ye stand there,
   Ye'll let yoursell down fa.'

And she gaed down, and farther down,
   Her love's ship for to see,
And the topmast and the mainmast
   Shone like the silver free.

And she's gane down, and farther down,
   The bride's ship to behold,
And the topmast and the mainmast
   They shone just like the gold.

She's taen her seven sons in her hand,
 I wot she didna fail;
She met Lord Thomas and his bride,
 As they came oer the dale.

'You're welcome to your house, Lord Thomas,
 You're welcome to your land;
You're welcome with your fair ladye,
 That you lead by the hand.

'You're welcome to your ha's, ladye,
 You're welcome to your bowers;
You're welcome to your hame, ladye,
 For a' that's here is yours.'

'I thank thee, Annie; I thank thee, Annie,
 Sae dearly as I thank thee;
You're the likest to my sister Annie,
 That ever I did see.

'There came a knight out oer the sea,
 And steald my sister away;
The shame scoup in his company,
 And land whereer he gae!'

She hang ae napkin at the door,
 Another in the ha,
And a' to wipe the trickling tears,
 Sae fast as they did fa.

And aye she served the lang tables,
 With white bread and with wine,
And aye she drank the wan water,
 To had her colour fine.

And aye she served the lang tables,
   With white bread and with brown;
And ay she turned her round about,
   Sae fast the tears fell down.

And he's taen down the silk napkin,
   Hung on a silver pin,
And aye he wipes the tear trickling
   A' down her cheik and chin.

And aye he turn'd him round about,
   And smil'd amang his men;
Says, 'Like ye best the old ladye,
   Or her that's new come hame?'

When bells were rung, and mass was sung,
   And a' men bound to bed,
Lord Thomas and his new-come bride
   To their chamber they were gaed.

Annie made her bed a little forbye,
   To hear what they might say;
'And ever alas!' Fair Annie cried,
   'That I should see this day!

'Gin my seven sons were seven young rats,
   Running on the castle wa,
And I were a grey cat mysell,
   I soon would worry them a'.

'Gin my seven young sons were seven young hares,
   Running oer yon lilly lee,
And I were a grew hound mysell,
   Soon worried they a' should be.'

And wae and sad Fair Annie sat,
　　And drearie was her sang,
And ever, as she sobbd and grat,
　　'Wae to the man that did the wrang!'

'My gown is on,' said the new-come bride,
　　'My shoes are on my feet,
And I will to Fair Annie's chamber,
　　And see what gars her greet.

'What ails ye, what ails ye, Fair Annie,
　　That ye make sic a moan?
Has your wine barrels cast the girds,
　　Or is your white bread gone?

'O wha was't was your father, Annie,
　　Or wha was't was your mother?
And had ye ony sister, Annie,
　　Or had ye ony brother?'

'The Earl of Wemyss was my father,
　　The Countess of Wemyss my mother;
And a' the folk about the house
　　To me were sister and brother.'

'If the Earl of Wemyss was your father,
　　I wot sae was he mine;
And it shall not be for lack o gowd
　　That ye your love sall tine.

'For I have seven ships o mine ain,
　　A' loaded to the brim,
And I will gie them a' to thee,
　　Wi' four to thine eldest son:
But thanks to a' the powers in heaven
　　That I gae maiden hame!'

Child Waters

Childe Watters in his stable stoode,
  And stroaket his milke-white steede;
To him there came a ffaire young ladye
  As ere did weare womans weede.

Saies, 'Christ you save, good Chyld Waters!'
  Sayes, 'Christ you save and see!
My girdle of gold, which was too longe,
  Is now to short for mee.

'And all is with one chyld of yours,
  I feele sturre att my side;
My gowne of greene, it is to strayght;
  Before it was to wide.'

'If the child be mine, Faire Ellen,' he sayd,
  'Be mine, as you tell mee,
Take you Cheshire and Lancashire both,
  Take them your owne to bee.

'If the child be mine, Faire Ellen,' he sayd,
  'Be mine, as you doe sweare,
Take you Cheshire and Lancashire both,
  And make that child your heyre.'

Shee saies, 'I had rather have one kisse,
  Child Waters, of thy mouth,
Then I wold have Cheshire and Lancashire both,
  That lyes by north and south.

'And I had rather have a twinkling,
  Child Waters, of your eye,
Then I wold have Cheshire and Lancashire both,
  To take them mine oune to bee.'

'To-morrow, Ellen, I must forth ryde
    Soe farr into the north countrye;
The fairest lady that I can find,
    Ellen, must goe with mee.'
'And ever I pray you, Child Watters,
    Your footpage let me bee!'

'If you will my footpage be, Ellen,
    As you doe tell itt mee,
Then you must cutt your gownne of greene
    An inche above your knee.

'Soe must you doe your yellow lockes,
    Another inch above your eye;
You must tell noe man what is my name;
    My footpage then you shall bee.'

All this long day Child Waters rode,
    Shee ran bare foote by his side;
Yett was he never soe curteous a knight
    To say, 'Ellen, will you ryde?'

But all this day Child Waters rode,
    Shee ran barfoote thorow the broome;
Yett he was never soe curteous a knight
    As to say, 'Put on your shoone.'

'Ride softlye,' shee said, 'Child Waters;
    Why doe you ryde soe fast?
The child which is no mans but yours
    My bodye itt will burst.'

He sayes, 'Sees thou yonder water, Ellen,
    That flowes from banke to brim?'
'I trust to God, Child Waters,' shee said,
    You will never see mee swime.'

But when shee came to the waters side,
　　Shee sayled to the chinne:
'Except the lord of heaven be my speed,
　　Now must I learne to swime.'

The salt waters bare up Ellens clothes,
　　Our Ladye bare upp her chinne,
And Child Waters was a woe man, good Lord,
　　To see Faire Ellen swime.

And when shee over the water was,
　　Shee then came to his knee:
He said, 'Come hither, Faire Ellen,
　　Loe yonder what I see!

'Seest thou not yonder hall, Ellen?
　　Of redd gold shine the yates;
There's four and twenty fayre ladyes,
　　The fairest is my worldlye make.

'Seest thou not yonder hall, Ellen?
　　Of redd gold shineth the tower;
There is four and twenty ffaire ladyes,
　　The fairest is my paramoure.'

'I doe see the hall now, Child Waters,
　　That of redd gold shineth the tower;
God give good then of your selfe,
　　And of your worldlye make!

'I doe see the hall now, Child Waters,
　　That of redd gold shineth the tower;
God give good then of your selfe,
　　And of your paramoure!'

There were four and twenty ladyes
    Were playing att the ball,
And Ellen, was the ffairest ladye,
    Must bring his steed to the stall.

There were four and twenty faire ladyes
    Was playing att the chesse;
And Ellen, shee was the ffairest ladye,
    Must bring his horsse to grasse.

And then bespake Child Waters sister,
    And these were the words said shee:
'You have the prettyest ffootpage, brother,
    That ever I saw with mine eye;

'But that his belly it is soe bigg,
    His girdle goes wonderous hye;
And ever I pray you, Child Waters,
    Let him goe into the chamber with mee.'

'It is more meete for a little ffootpage,
    That has run through mosse and mire,
To take his supper upon his knee
    And sitt downe by the kitchin fyer,
Then to goe into the chamber with any ladye
    That weares soe rich attyre.

But when thé had supped every one,
    To bedd they took the way;
He sayd, 'Come hither, my little footpage,
    Harken what I doe say.

'And goe thee downe into yonder towne,
    And low into the street;
The fairest ladye that thou can find,
    Hyer her in mine armes to sleepe,

And take her up in thine armes two,
    For filinge of her feete.

Ellen is gone into the towne,
    And low into the streete;
The fairest ladye that shee cold find
    Shee hyred in his armes to sleepe,
And tooke her in her armes two,
    For filinge of her feete.

'I pray you now, good Child Waters,
    That I may creepe in att your bedds feete;
For there is noe place about this house
    Where I may say a sleepe.'

This night and itt drove on afterward
    Till itt was neere the day:
He sayd, 'Rise up, my little ffoote-page,
    And give my steed corne and hay;
And soe doe thou the good blacke oates,
    That he may carry me the better away.'

And up then rose Faire Ellen,
    And gave his steed corne and hay,
And soe shee did and the good blacke oates,
    That he might carry him the better away.

Shee layned her backe to the manger side,
    And greivouslye did groane;
And that beheard his mother deere,
    And heard her make her moane.

Shee said, 'Rise up, thou Child Waters,
    I think thou art a cursed man;

For yonder is a ghost in thy stable,
  That greivouslye doth groane,
Or else some woman laboures of child,
  Shee is soe woe begone.

But up then rose Child Waters,
  And did on his shirt of silke;
Then he put on his other clothes
  On his body as white as milke.

And when he came to the stable-dore,
  Full still that hee did stand,
That hee might heare now Faire Ellen,
  How shee made her monand.

Shee said, Lullabye, my owne deere child!
  Lullabye, deere child, deere!
I wold thy father were a king,
  Thy mother layd on a beere!

'Peace now,' he said, 'good Faire Ellen,
  And be of good cheere, I thee pray,
And the bridall and the churching both,
  They shall bee upon one day.'

Young Hunting

Light you down, light you down, love Henry, she said,
  And stay all night with me;
For I have a bed and a fireside too,
  And a candle burning bright.

I can't get down, nor I won't get down
  And stay all night with thee,
For that little girl in the old Declarn
  Would think so hard of me.

TRADITIONAL

I will get down and I can get down
  And stay all night with thee,
For there's no little girl in the old Declarn
  That I love any better than thee.

But he slided down from his saddle skirts
  For to kiss her snowy white cheek,
She had a sharp knife in her hand,
  And she plunged it in him deep.

Must I ride to the East, must I ride to the West,
  Or anywhere under the sun,
To get some good and clever doctor
  For to cure this wounded man?

Neither ride to the East, neither ride to the West,
  Nor nowhere under the sun,
For there's no man but God's own hand
  Can cure this wounded man.

She took him by the long, yellow locks
  And also round the feet;
She plunged him into that doleful well,
  Some sixty fathoms deep.

And as she turned round to go home,
  She heard some pretty bird sing:
Go home, go home, you cruel girl,
  Lament and mourn for him.

Fly down, fly down, pretty parrot, she said,
  Fly down and go home with me.
Your cage shall be decked with beads of gold
  And hung in the willow tree.

I won't fly down, nor I can't fly down,
    And I won't go home with thee,
For you have murdered your own true love,
    And you might murder me.

I wish I had my little bow-ben
    And had it with a string;
I'd surely shoot that cruel bird
    That sits on the briers and sings.

I wish you had your little bow-ben
    And had it with a string;
I'd surely fly from vine to vine;
    You could always hear me sing.

Clerk Saunders

Clerk Saunders and a gay lady
    Was walking in yonder green,
And heavy, heavy was the love
    That fell this twa lovers between.

'A bed, a bed,' Clerk Saunders said,
    'And ay a bed for you and me;'
'Never a ane,' said the gay lady,
    'Till ance we twa married be.

'O I have seven bold brethren,
    And they are all valiant men,
If they knew a man that would tread my bower
    His life should not go along wi him.'

'Then take me up into your arms,
    And lay me low down on your bed,
That ye may swear, and keep your oath clear,
    That your bower-room I did na tread.

'Tie a handkerchief round your face,
   And you must tye it wondrous keen,
That you may swear, and keep your oath clear,
   Ye saw na me since late yestreen.'

But they were scarsley gone to bed,
   Nor scarse fa'n owre asleep,
Till up and started her seven brethren,
   Just at Lord Saunders' feet.

Out bespoke the first brither,
   'Oh but love be wondrous keen!'
Out bespoke the second brither,
   'It's ill done to kill a sleeping man.'

Out bespoke the third brither,
   'We had better gae and let him be;'
Out bespoke the fourth brither,
   'He'll no be killed this night for me;'

Out bespoke the fifth brither,
   'This night Lord Saunders he shall die;
Tho there were not a man in all Scotland,
   This night Lord Saunders he shall die.'

He took out a rusty rapier,
   And he drew it three times thro the strae;
Between Lord Saunders' short rib and his side
   He gard the rusty rapier gae.

'Awake, awake, Lord Saunders,' she said,
   'Awake, awake, for sin and shame!
For the day is light, and the sun shines bricht,
   And I am afraid we will be taen.

'Awake, awake, Lord Saunders,' she said,
  'Awake, awake, for sin and shame!
For the sheets they are asweat,' she said,
  'And I am afraid we will be taen.

'I dreamed a dreary dream last night,
  I wish it may be for our good,
That I was cutting my yellow hair,
  And dipping it in the wells o blood.'

Aye she waukened at this dead man,
  Aye she put on him to and fro;
Oh aye she waukened at this dead man,
  But of his death she did not know.

'It's I will do for my love's sake
  What many ladies would think lang;
Seven years shall come and go
  Before a glove go on my hand.

'And I will do for my love's sake
  What many ladies would not do;
Seven years shall come and go
  Before I wear stocking or shoe.

'There'll neer a shirt go on my back,
  There'll neer a kame go in my hair,
There'll never coal nor candle-light
  Shine in my bower nae mair.'

The Wife of Usher's Well

There lived a wife at Usher's Well,
  And a wealthy wife was she;
She had three stout and stalwart sons,
  And sent them o'er the sea.

TRADITIONAL

They hadna been a week from her,
  A week but barely ane,
Whan word came to the carline wife
  That her three sons were gane.

They hadna been a week from her,
  A week but barely three,
Whan word came to the carlin wife
  That her sons she'd never see.

'I wish the wind may never cease,
  Nor fashes in the flood,
Till my three sons come hame to me,
  In earthly flesh and blood.'

It fell about the Martinmass,
  When nights are lang and mirk,
The carlin wife's three sons came hame,
  And their hats were o' the birk.

It neither grew in syke nor ditch,
  Nor yet in ony sheugh;
But at the gates o Paradise,
  That birk grew fair eneugh.

'Blow up the fire, my maidens!
  Bring water from the well!
For a' my house shall feast this night,
  Since my three sons are well.'

And she has made to them a bed,
  She's made it large and wide,
And she's ta'en her mantle her about,
  Sat down at the bed-side.

Up then crew the red, red cock,
And up and crew the gray;
The eldest to the youngest said,
''Tis time we were away.'

The cock he hadna craw'd but once,
And clapp'd his wings at a',
When the youngest to the eldest said,
'Brother, we must awa'.

'The cock doth craw, the day doth daw,
The channerin' worm doth chide;
Gin we be mist out o' our place,
A sair pain we maun bide.

Fare ye weel, my mother dear!
Fareweel to barn and byre!
And fare ye weel, the bonny lass
That kindles my mother's fire!'

Little Musgrave and Lady Barnard

As it fell one holy-day,
Hay downe
As many be in the yeare,
When young men and maids together did goe,
Their mattins and masse to heare,

Little Musgrave came to the church-dore;
The preist was at private masse;
But he had more minde of the faire women
Then he had of Our Lady's grace.

The one of them was clad in green,
  Another was clad in pall,
And then came in my lord Bernard's wife,
  The fairest amonst them all.

She cast an eye on Little Musgrave,
  As bright as the summer sun;
And then bethought this Little Musgrave,
  This lady's heart have I woonn.

Quoth she, 'I have loved thee, Little Musgrave,
  Full long and many a day;'
'So have I loved you, fair lady,
  Yet never word durst I say.'

'I have a bower at Buckelsfordbery,
  Full daintyly it is deight;
If thou wilt wend thither, thou Little Musgrave,
  Thou's lig in mine armes all night.'

Quoth he, 'I thank yee, faire lady,
  This kindnes thou showest to me;
But whether it be to my weal or woe,
  This night I will lig with thee.'

With that he heard, a little tynë page,
  By his ladye's coach as he ran:
'All though I am my ladye's foot-page,
  Yet I am Lord Barnard's man.

'My lord Barnard shall knowe of this,
  Whether I sink or swim;'
And ever where the bridges were broake
  He laid him downe to swimme.

'A sleepe or wake, thou Lord Barnard,
    As thou art a man of life,
For Little Musgrave is at Bucklesfordbery,
    A bed with thy own wedded wife.'

'If this be true, thou little tinny page,
    This thing thou tellest to me,
Then all the land in Bucklesfordbery
    I freely will give to thee.

'But if it be a ly, thou little tinny page,
    This thing thou tellest to me,
On the hyest tree in Bucklesfordbery
    Then hanged shalt thou be.'

He called up his merry men all:
    'Come saddle me my steed;
This night must I to Buckellsfordbery,
    For I never had greater need.'

And some of them whistld, and some of them sung,
    And some these words did say,
And ever when my lord Barnard's horn blew,
    'Away, Musgrave, away!'

'Methinks I hear the thresel-cock,
    Methinks I hear the jaye;
Methinks I hear my lord Barnard,
    And I would I were away.'

'Lye still, lye still, thou Little Musgrave,
    And huggell me from the cold;
'Tis nothing but a shephard's boy,
    A driving his sheep to the fold.

'Is not thy hawke upon a perch?
   Thy steed eats oats and hay;
And thou a fair lady in thine armes,
   And wouldst thou bee away?'

With that my lord Barnard came to the dore,
   And lit a stone upon;
He plucked out three silver keys,
   And he opend the dores each one.

He lifted up the coverlett,
   He lifted up the sheet:
'How now, thou Littell Musgrave,
   Doest thou find my lady sweet?'

'I find her sweet,' quoth Little Musgrave,
   'The more 'tis to my paine;
I would gladly give three hundred pounds
   That I were on yonder plaine.'

'Arise, arise, thou Littell Musgrave,
   And put thy clothës on;
It shall nere be said in my country
   I have killed a naked man.

'I have two swords in one scabberd,
   Full deere they cost my purse;
And thou shalt have the best of them,
   And I will have the worse.'

The first stroke that Little Musgrave stroke,
   He hurt Lord Barnard sore;
The next stroke that Lord Barnard stroke,
   Little Musgrave nere struck more.

With that bespake the faire lady,
   In bed whereas she lay:
'Although thou'rt dead, thou Little Musgrave,
   Yet I for thee will pray.

'And wish well to thy soule will I,
   So long as I have life;
So will I not for thee, Barnard,
   Although I am thy wedded wife.'

He cut her paps from off her brest;
   Great pitty it was to see
That some drops of this ladie's heart's blood
   Ran trickling downe her knee.

'Woe worth you, woe worth, my mery men all,
   You were nere borne for my good;
Why did you not offer to stay my hand,
   When you see me wax so wood?

'For I have slaine the bravest sir knight
   That ever rode on steed;
So have I done the fairest lady
   That ever did woman's deed.

'A grave, a grave,' Lord Barnard cryd,
   'To put these lovers in;
But lay my lady on the upper hand,
   For she came of the better kin.'

Lamkin

It's Lamkin was a mason good as ever built wi' stane;
He built Lord Wearie's castle, but payment got he nane.

'O pay me, Lord Wearie, come, pay me my fee:'
'I canna pay you, Lamkin, for I maun gang o'er the sea.'

'O pay me now, Lord Wearie, come, pay me out o' hand:'
'I canna pay you, Lamkin, unless I sell my land.'

'O gin ye winna pay me, I here sall mak a vow,
Before that ye come hame again, ye sall ha'e cause to rue.'

Lord Wearie's got a bonny ship, to sail the saut sea faem;
Bade his lady weel the castle keep, ay till he should come hame.

But the nourice was a fause limmer as e'er hung on a tree;
She laid a plot wi' Lamkin, whan her lord was o'er the sea.

She laid a plot wi' Lamkin, when the servants were awa',
Loot him in at a little shot-window, and brought him to the ha'.

'O where's a' the men o' this house, that ca' me Lamkin?'
'They're at the barn-well thrashing; 'twill be lang ere they come
in.'

'And whare's the women o' this house, that ca' me Lamkin?'
'They're at the far well washing; 'twill be night or they come
hame.'

'And whare's the bairns o' this house, that ca' me Lamkin?'
'They're at the school reading; 'twill be night or they come
hame.'

'O whare's the lady o' this house, that ca's me Lamkin?'
'She's up in her bower sewing, but we soon can bring her down.'

Then Lamkin's tane a sharp knife, that hang down by his gaire,
And he has gi'en the bonny babe a deep wound and a sair.

Then Lamkin he rocked, and the fause nourice sang,
Till frae ilka bore o' the cradle the red blood out sprang.

Then out it spak the lady, as she stood on the stair:
'What ails my bairn, nourice, that he's greeting sae sair?'

'O still my bairn, nourice, O still him wi' the pap!'
'He winna still, lady, for this nor for that.'

'O still my bairn, nourice, O still him wi' the wand!'
'He winna still, lady, for a' his father's land.'

'O still my bairn, nourice, O still him wi' the bell!'
'He winna still, lady, till ye come down yoursel.'

O the firsten step she steppit, she steppit on a stane;
But the neisten step she steppit, she met him Lamkin.

'O mercy, mercy, Lamkin, ha'e mercy upon me!
Though you've ta'en my young son's life, ye may let mysel be.'

'O sall I kill her, nourice, or sall I let her be?'
'O kill her, kill her, Lamkin, for she ne'er was good to me.'

'O scour the bason, nourice, and mak it fair and clean,
For to keep this lady's heart's blood, for she's come o' noble
    kin.'

'There need nae bason, Lamkin, lat it run through the floor;
What better is the heart's blood o' the rich than o' the poor?'

But ere three months were at an end, Lord Wearie came again;
But dowie, dowie was his heart when first he came hame.

'O wha's blood is this,' he says, 'that lies in the chamer?'
'It is your lady's heart's blood; 'tis as clear as the lamer.'

'And wha's blood is this,' he says, 'that lies in my ha'?'
'It is your young son's heart's blood; 'tis the clearest ava.'

O sweetly sang the black-bird that sat upon the tree;
But sairer grat Lamkin, when he was condemnd to die.

And bonny sang the mavis, out o' the thorny brake;
But sairer grat the nourice, when she was tied to the stake.

The Bailiff's Daughter of Islington

There was a youthe, and a well-beloved youthe,
    And he was a squire's son:
He loved the bayliffe's daughter deare,
    That lived in Islington.

Yet she was coye and would not believe,
    That he did love her soe,
Noe nor at any time would she
    Any countenance to him showe.

But when his friendes did understand
    His fond and foolish minde,
They sent him up to faire London
    An apprentice for to binde.

And he had been seven long yeares,
    And never his love could see:
'Many a teare have I shed for her sake,
    When she little thought of mee.'

Then all the maids of Islington
    Went forth to sport and playe,
All but the bayliffe's daughter deare;
    She secretly stole awaye.

She pulled off her gowne of greene,
    And put on ragged attire,
And to faire London she would go
    Her true love to enquire.

And as she went along the high road,
　The weather being hot and drye,
She sat her downe upon a green bank,
　And her true love came riding bye.

She started up, with a colour soe redd,
　Catching hold of his bridle-reine;
'One penny, one penny, kind sir,' she sayd,
　'Will ease me of much paine.'

'Before I give you one penny, sweet-heart,
　Praye tell me where you were borne.'
'At Islington, kind sir,' sayd shee,
　'Where I have had many a scorne.'

'I prythee, sweet-heart, then tell to mee,
　O tell me, whether you knowe
The bayliffe's daughter of Islington.'
　'She is dead, sir, long agoe.'

'If she be dead, then take my horse,
　My saddle and bridle also;
For I will into some farr countrye,
　Where noe man shall me knowe.'

'O staye, O staye, thou goodlye youthe,
　She standeth by thy side;
She is here alive, she is not dead,
　And readye to be thy bride.'

'O farewell griefe, and welcome joye,
　Ten thousand times therefore;
For nowe I have founde mine owne true love,
　Whom I thought I should never see more.'

The Great Silkie of Sule Skerry

An eartly nourris sits and sings,
    And aye she sings, 'Ba, lily wean!
Little ken I my bairnis father,
    Far less the land that he staps in.'

Then ane arose at her bed-fit,
    An' a grumly guest I'm sure was he:
'Here am I, thy bairnis father,
    Although that I be not comelie.

'I am a man, upo the lan,
    An' I am a silkie in the sea;
And when I'm far and far frae lan,
    My dwelling is in Sule Skerrie.'

'It was na weel,' quo the maiden fair,
    'It was na weel, indeed,' quo she,
That the Great Silkie of Sule Skerrie
    Suld hae come and aught a bairn to me.'

Now he has taen a purse of goud,
    And he has pat it upo her knee,
Sayin, 'Gie to me my little young son,
    An' tak thee up thy nourris-fee.

'An' it sall come to pass on a simmer's day,
    When the sin shines het on evera stane,
That I will tak my little young son,
    An' teach him for to swim the faem.

'An' thu sall marry a proud gunner,
    An' a proud gunner I'm sure he'll be,
An' the very first schot that ere he schoots,
    He'll schoot baith my young son and me.'

Sir Hugh
(*The Jew's Daughter*)

Four and twenty bonny boys
    Were playing at the ba,
And by it came him, sweet Sir Hugh,
    And he played o'er them a.

He kick'd the ba with his right foot,
    And catchd it wi' his knee,
And throuch-and-thro the Jew's window
    He gard the bonny ba flee.

He's doen him to the Jew's castell,
    And walkd it round about;
And there he saw the Jew's daughter,
    At the window looking out.

'Throw down the ba, ye Jew's daughter,
    Throw down the ba to me!'
'Never a bit,' says the Jew's daughter,
    'Till up to me come ye.'

'How will I come up? How can I come up?
    How can I come to thee?
For as ye did to my auld father,
    The same ye'll do to me.'

She's gane till her father's garden,
    And pu'd an apple red and green,
'Twas a' to wyle him, sweet Sir Hugh,
    And to entice him in.

70

She's led him in through ae dark door,
    And sae has she thro' nine;
She's laid him on a dressing-table,
    And stickit him like a swine.

And first came out the thick, thick blood,
    And syne came out the thin;
And syne came out the bonny heart's blood;
    There was nae mair within.

She's row'd him in a cake o' lead,
    Bade him lie still and sleep;
She's thrown him in Our Lady's draw-well.
    Was fifty fathom deep.

When the bells were rung, and mass was sung,
    And a' the bairns came hame,
When every lady gat hame her son,
    The Lady Maisry gat nane.

She's ta'en her mantle her about,
    Her coffer by the hand,
And she's gane out to seek her son,
    And wanderd oer the land.

She's doen her to the Jew's castell,
    Where a' were fast asleep:
'Gin ye be there, my sweet Sir Hugh,
    I pray you to me speak.'

She's doen her to the Jew's garden,
    Thought he had been gathering fruit:
'Gin ye be there, my sweet Sir Hugh,
    I pray you to me speak.'

'Gae hame, gae hame, my mither dear,
   Prepare my winding sheet,
And at the back o' merry Lincoln
   The morn I will you meet.'

Now Lady Maisry is gane hame,
   Made him a winding sheet,
And at the back o' merry Lincoln
   The dead corpse did her meet.

And a' the bells o' merry Lincoln
   Without men's hands were rung;
And a' the books o' merry Lincoln
   Were read without man's tongue;
And ne'er was such a burial
   Sin Adam's days begun.

The Gypsy Laddie

The gypsies they came to my lord Cassilis' yett,
   And O but they sang bonnie!
They sang so sweet and so complete
   Till down came our fair ladie.

She came tripping down the stairs,
   And all her maids before her;
As soon as they saw her weel-far'd face,
   They cast their glamourie owre her.

She gave them the good wheat bread,
   And they gave her the ginger;
But she gave them a fair better thing,
   The gold rings of her fingers.

'Will ye go with me, my hinny and my heart?
  Will you go with me, my dearie?
And I will swear by the hilt of my spear,
  That your lord shall no more come near thee.'

'Gar take from me my silk manteel,
  And bring to me a plaidie,
For I will travel the world owre
  Along with the gypsie laddie.

'I could sail the seas with my Jackie Faa,
  I could sail the seas with my dearie;
I could sail the seas with my Jackie Faa,
  And with pleasure could drown with my dearie.'

They wandred high, they wandred low,
  They wandred late and early,
Untill they came to an old farmer's barn,
  And by this time she was weary.

'Last night I lay in a weel-made bed,
  And my noble lord beside me,
And now I most ly in an old farmer's barn,
  And the black crae glowring owre me.'

'Hold your tongue, my hinny and my heart,
  Hold your tongue, my dearie,
For I will swear, by the moon and the stars,
  That thy lord shall no more come near thee.'

They wandred high, they wandred low,
  They wandred late and early,
Untill they came to that on water,
  And by this time she was wearie.

'Many a time I have rode that on water,
  And my lord Cassilis beside me,
And now I must set in my white feet and wade,
  And carry the gypsie laddie.'

By and by came home this noble lord,
  And asking for his ladie,
The one did cry, the other did reply,
  'She is gone with the gypsie laddie.'

'Go saddle to me the black,' he says,
  'The brown rides never so speedie,
And I will neither eat nor drink
  Till I bring home my ladie.'

He wandred high, he wandred low,
  He wandred late and early,
Untill he came to that on water,
  And there he spied his ladie.

'O wilt thou go home, my hinny and my heart,
  O wilt thou go home, my dearie?
And I'll close thee in a close room,
  Where no man shall come near thee.'

'I will not go home, my hinny and my heart,
  I will not go home, my dearie;
If I have brewn good beer, I will drink of the same,
  And my lord shall no more come near me.

'But I will swear, by the moon and the stars,
  And the sun that shines so clearly,
That I am as free of the gypsie gang
  As the hour my mother bore me.'

They were fifteen valiant men,
    Black, but very bonny,
They lost all their lives for one,
    The Earl of Cassillis' ladie.

James Harris
(*The Demon Lover*)

'O where have you been, my long, long love,
    This long seven years and mair?'
'O I'm come to seek my former vows
    Ye granted me before.'

'O hold your tongue of your former vows,
    For they will breed sad strife;
O hold your tongue of your former vows,
    For I am become a wife.'

He turned him right and round about,
    And the tear blinded his ee:
'I wad never hae trodden on Irish ground,
    If it had not been for thee.

'I might hae had a king's daughter,
    Far, far beyond the sea;
I might have had a king's daughter,
    Had it not been for love o thee.'

'If ye might have had a king's daughter,
    Yer sel ye had to blame;
Ye might have taken the king's daughter,
    For ye kend that I was nane.

'If I was to leave my husband dear,
    And my two babes also,
O what have you to take me to,
    If with you I should go?'

TRADITIONAL

'I hae seven ships upon the sea—
     The eighth brought me to land—
With four-and-twenty bold mariners,
     And music on every hand.'

She has taken up her two little babes,
     Kiss'd them baith cheek and chin:
'O fair ye weel, my ain two babes,
     For I'll never see you again.'

She set her foot upon the ship,
     No mariners could she behold;
But the sails were o the taffetie,
     And the masts o the beaten gold.

They had not sailed a league, a league,
     A league but barely three,
When dismal grew his countenance,
     And drumlie grew his ee.

They had not sailed a league, a league,
     A league but barely three,
Until she espied his cloven foot,
     And she wept right bitterlie.

'O hold your tongue of your weeping,' says he,
     'Of your weeping now let me be;
I will shew you how lilies grow
     On the banks of Italy.'

'O what hills are yon, yon pleasant hills,
     That the sun shines sweetly on?'
'O yon are the hills of heaven,' he said,
     'Where you will never win.'

'O whaten mountain is yon,' she said,
  'All so dreary wi frost and snow?'
'O yon is the mountain of hell,' he cried
  'Where you and I will go.'

He strack the tap-mast wi his hand,
  The fore-mast wi his knee,
And he brake that gallant ship in twain,
  And sank her in the sea.

Get Up and Bar the Door

It fell about the Martinmas time,
  And a gay time it was then,
When our goodwife got puddings to make,
  And she's boild them in the pan.

The wind sae cauld blew south and north,
  And blew into the floor;
Quoth our goodman to our goodwife,
  'Gae out and bar the door.'

'My hand is in my hussyfskap,
  Goodman, as ye may see;
An it should nae be barrd this hundred year,
  It's no be barrd for me.'

They made a paction tween them twa,
  They made it firm and sure,
That the first word whaeer shoud speak,
  Shoud rise and bar the door.

Then by there came two gentlemen,
  At twelve o clock at night,
And they could neither see house nor hall,
  Nor coal nor candle-light.

'Now whether is this a rich man's house,
    Or whether is it a poor?'
But neer a word wad ane o them speak,
    For barring of the door.

And first they ate the white puddings,
    And then they ate the black;
Tho muckle thought the goodwife to hersel,
    Yet neer a word she spake.

Then said the one unto the other,
    'Here, man, tak ye my knife;
Do ye tak aff the auld man's beard,
    And I'll kiss the goodwife.'

'But there's nae water in the house,
    And what shall we do than?'
'What ails ye at the pudding-broo,
    That boils into the pan?'

O up then started our goodman,
    An angry man was he:
'Will ye kiss my wife before my een,
    And scad me wi pudding-bree?'

Then up and started our goodwife,
    Gied three skips on the floor:
'Goodman, you've spoken the foremost word,
    Get up and bar the door.'

II

Robin Hood and Border Ballads

Robin Hood and the Monk

In somer, when the shawes be sheyne,
  And leves be large and long,
Hit is full mery in feyre foreste
  To here the foulys song:

To se the dere draw to the dale,
  And leve the hilles hee,
And shadow hem in the levës grene,
  Under the grene-wode tre.

Hit befel on Whitsontide,
  Erly in a May mornyng,
The son up feyre can shyne,
  And the birddis mery can syng.

'This is a mery mornyng,' seid Litull John,
  'Be hym that dyed on tre;
A more mery man then I am one
  Lyves not in Cristiantë.

'Pluk up thi hert, my dere mayster,'
  Litull John can sey,
'And thynk hit is a full fayre tyme
  In a mornyng of May.'

'Yea, on thyng greves me,' seid Robyn,
  'And does my hert mych woo;
That I may not no solem day
  To mas nor matyns goo.

'Hit is a fourtnet and more,' seid he,
  'Syn I my savyour see;

To-day wil I to Notyngham,' seid Robyn,
  'With the myght of mylde Marye.'

Than spake Moche, the mylner sun,
  Ever more wel hym betyde!
'Take twelve of thi wyght yemen,
  Well weppynd, be thi side.
Such on wolde thi selfe slon,
  That twelve dar not abyde.'

'Of all my mery men,' seid Robyn,
  'Be my feith I wil non have,
But Litull John shall beyre my bow,
  Til that me list to drawe.'

'Thou shall beyre thin own,' seid Litull Jon,
  'Maister, and I wyl beyre myne,
And we well shete a peny,' seid Litull Jon,
  'Under the grene-wode lyne.'

'I wil not shete a peny,' seyd Robyn Hode,
  'In feith, Litull John, with the,
But ever for on as thou shetis,' seide Robyn,
  'In feith I holde the thre.'

Thus shet thei forth, these yemen too,
  Bothe at buske and brome,
Til Litull John wan of his maister
  Five shillings to hose and shone.

A ferly strife fel them betwene,
  As they went bi the way;
Litull John seid he had won five shillings,
  And Robyn Hode seid schortly nay.

With that Robyn Hode lyed Litul Jon,
   And smote hym with his hande;
Litul Jon waxed wroth therwith,
   And pulled out his bright bronde.

'Were thou not my maister,' sed Litull John,
   'Thou shuldis by hit ful sore;
Get the a man wher thou wilt,
   For thou getis me no more.'

Then Robyn goes to Notyngham,
   Hym selfe mornyng allone,
And Litull John to mery Scherwode,
   The pathes he knew ilkone.

Whan Robyn came to Notyngham,
   Sertenly withouten layn,
He prayed to God and myld Mary
   To bryng hym out save agayn.

He gos in to Seynt Mary chirch,
   And kneled down before the rode;
Alle that ever were the church within
   Beheld wel Robyn Hode.

Beside hym stod a gret-hedid munke,
   I pray to God woo he be!
Fful sone he knew gode Robyn,
   As sone as he hym se.

Out at the durre he ran,
   Fful sone and anon;
Alle the yatis of Notyngham
   He made to be sparred everychon.

'Rise up,' he seid, 'thou prowde schereff,
    Buske the and make the bowne;
I have spyed the kynggis felon,
    Ffor sothe he is in this town.

'I have spyed the false felon,
    As he stondis at his masse;
Hit is long of the,' seid the munke,
    'And ever he fro us passe.

'This traytur name is Robyn Hode,
    Under the grene-wode lynde;
He robbyt me onys of a hundred pound,
    Hit shalle never out of my mynde.'

Up then rose this prowde shereff,
    And radly made him yare;
Many was the moder son
    To the kyrk with hym can fare.

In at the durres thei throly thrast,
    With staves ful gode wone;
'Alas, alas!' seid Robyn Hode,
    'Now misse I Litull John.'

But Robyn toke out a too-hond sworde,
    That hangit down be his kne;
Ther as the schereff and his men stode thyckust,
    Thedurwarde wolde he.

Thryes thorowout them he ran then,
    For sothe as I yow sey,
And woundyt mony a moder son,
    And twelve he slew that day.

His sworde upon the schireff hed
   Sertanly he brake in too;
'The smyth that the made,' seid Robyn,
   'I pray to God wyrke hym woo!

'Ffor now am I weppynlesse,' seid Robyn,
   'Alasse! agayn my wylle;
But if I may fle these traytors fro,
   I wot thei wil me kyll.'

Robyn in to the churchë ran,
   Throout hem everilkon,

     ★   ★   ★   ★   ★

     [*News of Robin's capture*]
Sum fel in swonyng as thei were dede,
   And lay stil as any stone;
Non of theym were in her mynde
   But only Litull Jon.

'Let be your rule,' seid Litull Jon,
   'Ffor his luf that dyed on tre,
Ye that shulde be dughty men;
   Het is gret shame to se.

'Oure maister has bene hard bystode
   And yet scapyd away;
Pluk up your hertis, and leve this mone,
   And harkyn what I shal say.

'He has servyd Oure Lady many a day,
   And yet wil, securly;
Therfor I trust in hir specialy
   No wyckud deth shal he dye.

'Therfor be glad,' seid Litul John,
  'And let this mournyng be;
And I shal be the munkis gyde,
  With the myght of mylde Mary.

★　★　★　★　★

  'We will go but we too;
And I mete hym,' seid Litul John,

★　★　★　★　★

'Loke that ye kepe wel owre tristil-tre,
  Under the levys smale,
And spare non of this venyson,
  That gose in thys vale.'

Fforthe then went these yemen too,
  Litul John and Moche on fere,
And lokid on Moch emys hows,
  The hye way lay full nere.

Litul John stode at a wyndow in the mornyng,
  And lokid forth at a stage;
He was war wher the munke came ridyng,
  And with hym a litul page.

'Be my feith,' seid Litul John to Moch,
  'I can the tel tithyngus gode;
I se wher the munke cumys rydyng,
  I know hym be his wyde hode.'

They went in to the way, these yemen bothe,
  As curtes men and hende;
Thei spyrred tithyngus at the munke,
  As they hade bene his frende.

'Ffro whens come ye?' seid Litull Jon,
  'Tel us tithyngus, I yow pray,
Off a false owtlay, callid Robyn Hode,
  Was takyn yisterday.

'He robbyt me and my felowes bothe
  Of twenti marke in serten;
If that false owtlay be takyn,
  Ffor sothe we wolde be fayn.'

'So did he me,' seid the munke,
  'Of a hundred pound and more;
I layde furst hande hym apon,
  Ye may thonke me therfore.'

'I pray God thanke you,' seid Litull John,
  'And we wil when we may;
We wil go with you, with your leve,
  And bryng yow on your way.

'Ffor Robyn Hode hase many a wilde felow,
  I tell you in certen;
If thei wist ye rode this way,
  In feith ye shulde be slayn.'

As thei went talking be the way,
  The munke and Litull John,
John toke the munkis horse be the hede,
  Fful sone and anon.

Johne toke the munkis horse be the hed,
  Ffor sothe as I yow say;
So did Much the litull page,
  Ffor he sulde not scape away.

Be the golett of the hode
　　John pulled the munke down;
John was nothyng of hym agast,
　　He lete hym falle on his crown.

Litull John was sore agreyvd,
　　And drew out his swerde in hye;
This munke saw he shulde be ded,
　　Lowd mercy can he crye.

'He was my maister,' seid Litull John,
　　'That thou hase browght in bale;
Shalle thou never cum at our kyng,
　　Ffor to telle hym tale.'

John smote of the munkis hed,
　　No longer wolde he dwell;
So did Moch the litull page,
　　Ffor ferd lest he wolde tell.

Ther thei beryed hem bothe,
　　In nouther mosse nor lyng,
And Litull John and Much infere
　　Bare the letturs to oure kyng.

　　　*　　*　　*　　*　　*

He knelid down upon his kne:
'God yow save, my lege lorde,
　　Ihesus yow save and se!

'God yow save, my lege kyng!'
　　To speke John was full bolde;
He gaf hym the letturs in his hond,
　　The kyng did hit unfold.

The kyng red the letturs anon,
　And seid, 'So mot I the,
Ther was never yoman in mery Inglond
　I longut so sore to se.

'Wher is the munke that these shuld have brouyt ?'
　Oure kyng can say:
'Be my trouth,' seid Litull John,
　'He dyed after the way.'

The kyng gaf Moch and Litul Jon
　Twenti pound in sertan,
And made theim yemen of the crown,
　And bade theim go agayn.

He gaf John the seel in hand,
　The sheref for to bere,
To bryng Robyn hym to,
　And no man do hym dere.

John toke his leve at oure kyng,
　The sothe as I yow say;
The next way to Notyngham
　To take, he yede the way.

Whan John came to Notyngham
　The yatis were sparred ychon;
John callid up the porter,
　He answerid sone anon.

'What is the cause,' seid Litul Jon,
　'Thou sparris the yates so fast ?'
'Because of Robyn Hode,' seid the porter,
　'In depe prison is cast.

'John and Moch and Wyll Scathlok,
    Ffor sothe as I yow say,
Thei slew oure men upon our wallis,
    And sawten vs every day.'

Litull John spyrred after the schereff,
    And sone he hym fonde;
He oppyned the kyngus prive seell,
    And gaf hym in his honde.

Whan the scheref saw the kyngus seell,
    He did of his hode anon;
'Where is the munke that bare the letturs?'
    He seid to Litull John.

'He is so fayn of hym,' seid Litul John,
    'Ffor sothe as I yow say,
He has made hym abot of Westmynster,
    A lorde of that abbay.'

The scheref made John gode chere,
    And gaf hym wyne of the best;
At nyght thei went to her bedde,
    And every man to his rest.

When the scheref was on slepe,
    Dronken of wyne and ale,
Litul John and Moch for sothe,
    Toke the way unto the jale.

Litul John callid up the jayler,
    And bade hym rise anon;
He seyd Robyn Hode had brokyn prison,
    And out of hit was gon.

The porter rose anon sertan,
    As sone as he herd John calle;
Litul John was redy with a swerd,
    And bare hym to the walle.

'Now wil I be porter,' seid Litul John,
    'And take the keyes in honde:'
He toke the way to Robyn Hode,
    And sone he hym unbonde.

He gaf hym a gode swerd in his hond,
    His hed therwith for to kepe,
And ther as the walle was lowyst
    Anon down can thei lepe.

Be that the cok began to crow,
    The day began to spryng;
The scheref fond the jaylier ded,
    The comyn bell made he ryng.

He made a crye thoroout al the town,
    Wheder he be yoman or knave,
That cowthe bryng hym Robyn Hode,
    His warison he shuld have.

'Ffor I dar never,' said the scheref,
    'Cum before oure kyng;
Ffor if I do, I wot serten
    Ffor sothe he wil me heng.'

The scheref made to seke Notyngham,
    Bothe be strete and stye,
And Robyn was in mery Scherwode,
    As light as lef on lynde.

Then bespake gode Litull John,
    To Robyn Hode can he say,
'I have done the a gode turne for an evyll,
    Quyte the whan thou may.

'I have done the a gode turne,' seid Litull John,
    'Ffor sothe as I yow say;
I have brought the under grene-wode lyne;
    Ffare wel, and have gode day.'

'Nay, be my trouth,' seid Robyn Hode,
    'So shall hit never be;
I make the maister,' seid Robyn Hode,
    'Off alle my men and me.'

'Nay, be my trouth,' seid Litull John,
    'So shalle hit never be;
But lat me be a felow,' seid Litull John,
    'No noder kepe I be.'

Thus John gate Robyn Hod out of prison,
    Sertan withoutyn layn;
Whan his men saw hym hol and sounde,
    Ffor sothe they were full fayne.

They filled in wyne and made hem glad,
    Under the levys smale,
And yete pastes of venyson,
    That gode was with ale.

Than worde came to oure kyng
    How Robyn Hode was gon,
And how the scheref of Notyngham
    Durst never loke hym upon.

Then bespake oure cumly kyng,
    In an angur hye:
'Litull John hase begyled the schereff,
    In faith so hase he me.

'Litul John has begyled us bothe,
    And that full wel I se;
Or ellis the schereff of Notyngham
    Hye hongust shulde he be.

'I made hem yemen of the crowne,
    And gaf hem fee with my hond;
I gaf hem grith,' seid oure knyg,
    'Thorowout all mery Inglond.

'I gaf theym grith,' then seid oure kyng;
    'I say, so mot I the,
Ffor sothe soch a yemen as he is on
    In all Inglond ar not thre.

'He is trew to his maister,' seid our kyng;
    'I sey, be swete Seynt John,
He lovys better Robyn Hode
    Then he dose us ychon.

'Robyn Hode is ever bond to hym,
    Bothe in strete and stalle;
Speke no more of this matter,' seid oure kyng,
    'But John has begyled us alle.'

Thus endys the talkyng of the munke
    And Robyn Hode i-wysse;
God, that is ever a crowned kyng,
    Bryng us all to his blisse!

Robin Hood's Death

When Robin Hood and Little John
   Down a down a down a down
Went oer yon bank of broom,
   Said Robin Hood bold to Little John,
'We have shot for many a pound.
   Hey etc.

'But I am not able to shoot one shot more,
   My broad arrows will not flee;
But I have a cousin lives down below,
   Please God, she will bleed me.'

Now Robin he is to fair Kirkly gone,
   As fast as he can win;
But before he came there, as we do hear,
   He was taken very ill.

And when he came to fair Kirkly-hall,
   He knock'd all at the ring,
But none was so ready as his cousin herself
   For to let bold Robin in.

'Will you please to sit down, cousin Robin,' she said,
   'And drink some beer with me?'
'No, I will neither eat nor drink,
   Till I am blooded by thee.'

'Well, I have a room, cousin Robin,' she said,
   'Which you did never see,
And if you please to walk therein,
   You blooded by me shall be.'

She took him by the lily-white hand,
  And led him to a private room,
And there she blooded bold Robin Hood,
  While one drop of blood would run down.

She blooded him in a vein of the arm,
  And locked him up in the room;
Then did he bleed all the live-long day,
  Until the next day at noon.

He then bethought him of a casement there,
  Thinking for to get down;
But was so weak he could not leap,
  He could not get him down.

He then bethought him of his bugle-horn,
  Which hung low down to his knee;
He set his horn unto his mouth,
  And blew out weak blasts three.

Then Little John, when hearing him,
  As he sat under a tree,
'I fear my master is now near dead,
  He blows so wearily.'

Then Little John to fair Kirkly is gone,
  As fast as he can dree;
But when he came to Kirkly-hall,
  He broke locks two or three:

Until he came bold Robin to see,
  Then he fell on his knee;
'A boon, a boon,' cries Little John,
  'Master, I beg of thee.'

'What is that boon,' said Robin Hood,
    'Little John, thou begs of me?'
'It is to burn fair Kirkly-hall,
    And all their nunnery.'

'Now nay, now nay,' quoth Robin Hood,
    'That boon I'll not grant thee;
I never hurt woman in all my life,
    Nor men in woman's company.

'I never hurt fair maid in all my time,
    Nor at mine end shall it be;
But give me my bent bow in my hand,
    And a broad arrow I'll let flee;
And where this arrow is taken up,
    There shall my grave digged be.

'Lay me a green sod under my head,
    And another at my feet;
And lay my bent bow by my side,
    Which was my music sweet;
And make my grave of gravel and green,
    Which is most right and meet.

'Let me have length and breadth enough,
    With a green sod under my head;
That they may say, when I am dead
    Here lies bold Robin Hood.'

Chevy Chase
(*The Hunting of the Cheviot*)

God prosper long our noble king,
    Our liffes and saftyes all!
A woefull hunting once there did
    In Chevy Chase befall.

To drive the deere with hound and horne
    Erle Pearcy took the way:
The child may rue that is unborne
    The hunting of that day!

The stout Erle of Northumberland
    A vow to God did make
His pleasure in the Scottish woods
    Three sommers days to take,

The cheefest harts in Chevy Chase
    To kill and beare away:
These tydings to Erle Douglas came
    In Scottland where he lay.

Who sent Erle Pearcy present word
    He wold prevent his sport;
The English erle, not fearing that,
    Did to the woods resort,

With fifteen hundred bowmen bold,
    All chosen men of might,
Who knew ffull well in time of neede
    To ayme their shafts arright.

The gallant greyhounds swiftly ran
    To chase the fallow deere;
On Munday they began to hunt,
    Ere daylight did appeare.

And long before high noone they had
    A hundred fat buckes slaine;
Then having dined, the drovyers went
    To rouze the deare againe.

The bowmen mustered on the hills,
    Well able to endure;
Theire backsids all with speciall care
    That day were guarded sure.

The hounds ran swiftly through the woods
    The nimble deere to take,
That with their cryes the hills and dales
    An eccho shrill did make.

Lord Pearcy to the querry went
    To view the tender deere;
Quoth he, 'Erle Douglas promised once
    This day to meete me here;

'But if I thought he wold not come,
    Noe longer wold I stay.'
With that a brave younge gentlman
    Thus to the erle did say:

'Loe, yonder doth Erle Douglas come,
    Hys men in armour bright;
Full twenty hundred Scottish speres
    All marching in our sight.

'All men of pleasant Tivydale,
    Fast by the river Tweede:'
'O ceaze your sportts!' Erle Pearcy said,
    'And take your bowes with speede.

'And now with me, my countrymen,
    Your courage forth advance!
For there was never champion yett,
    In Scottland nor in Ffrance,

'That ever did on horsbacke come,
    But, if my hap it were,
I durst encounter man for man,
    With him to breake a spere.'

Erle Douglas on his milk-white steede,
    Most like a baron bold,
Rode formost of his company,
    Whose armor shone like gold.

'Shew me,' sayd hee, 'whose men you bee
    That hunt so boldly heere,
That without my consent doe chase
    And kill my fallow deere.'

The first man that did answer make
    Was noble Pearcy hee,
Who sayd, 'Wee list not to declare
    Nor shew whose men wee bee;

'Yett wee will spend our deerest blood
    Thy cheefest harts to slay.'
Then Douglas swore a solempne oathe,
    And thus in rage did say:

'Ere thus I will outbraved bee,
    One of us tow shall dye;
I know thee well, an erle thou art;
    Lord Pearcy, soe am I.

'But trust me, Pearcye, pittye it were,
    And great offence, to kill
Then any of these our guiltlesse men,
    For they have done none ill.

'Let thou and I the battell trye,
    And set our men aside:'
'Accurst bee he!' Erle Pearcye sayd,
    'By whome it is denyed.'

Then stept a gallant squire forth—
    Witherington was his name—
Who said, 'I wold not have it told
    To Henery our king, for shame,

'That ere my captaine fought on foote,
    And I stand looking on.
You bee two Erles,' quoth Witheringhton,
    'And I a squier alone;

'I'le doe the best that doe I may,
    While I have power to stand;
While I have power to weeld my sword,
    I'le fight with hart and hand.'

Our English archers bent their bowes;
    Their harts were good and trew;
Att the first flight of arrowes sent,
    Full foure score Scotts they slew.

To drive the deere with hound and horne,
    Dauglas bade on the bent;
Two captaines moved with mickle might,
    Their speres to shivers went.

They closed full fast on every side,
    Noe slackness there was found,
But many a gallant gentleman
    Lay gasping on the ground.

O Christ! it was great greeve to see
　How eche man chose his spere,
And how the blood out of their brests
　Did gush like water cleare.

At last these two stout erles did meet,
　Like captaines of great might;
Like lyons woode they layd on lode;
　They made a cruell fight.

They fought untill they both did sweat,
　With swords of tempered steele,
Till blood downe their cheekes like raine
　The trickling downe did feele.

'O yeeld thee, Pearcye!' Douglas sayd,
　'And in faith I will thee bringe
Where thou shall high advanced bee
　By James our Scottish king.

'Thy ransome I will freely give,
　And this report of thee,
Thou art the most couragious knight
　That ever I did see.'

'Noe, Douglas!' quoth Erle Percy then,
　'Thy profer I doe scorne;
I will not yeelde to any Scott
　That ever yett was borne!'

With that there came an arrow keene,
　Out of an English bow,
Which stroke Erle Douglas on the brest
　A deepe and deadlye blow.

Who never sayd more words than these:
   'Fight on, my merry men all!
For why, my life is att an end,
   Lord Pearcy sees my fall.'

Then leaving liffe, Erle Pearcy tooke
   The dead man by the hand;
Who said, 'Erle Dowglas, for thy life,
   Wold I had lost my hand;

'O Christ! my verry hart doth bleed
   For sorrow for thy sake,
For sure, a more redoubted knight
   Mischance could never take.'

A knight amongst the Scotts there was
   Which saw Erle Douglas dye,
Who streight in hart did vow revenge
   Upon the Lord Pearcye.

Sir Hugh Mountgomerye was he called,
   Who, with a spere full bright,
Well mounted on a gallant steed,
   Ran feircly through the fight,

And past the English archers all,
   Without all dread or feare,
And through Erle Percyes body then
   He thrust his hatfull spere.

With such a vehement force and might
   His body he did gore,
The staff ran through the other side
   A large cloth yard and more.

Thus did both those nobles dye,
　　Whose courage none cold staine;
An English archer then perceived
　　The noble erle was slaine.

He had a good bow in his hand,
　　Made of a trusty tree;
An arrow of a cloth yard long
　　To the hard head haled hee.

Against Sir Hugh Mountgomerye
　　His shaft full right he sett;
The grey goose winge that was there-on
　　In his harts bloode was wett.

This fight from breake of day did last
　　Till setting of the sun,
For when they rung the evening-bell
　　The battele scarse was done.

With stout Erle Percy there was slaine
　　Sir John of Egerton,
Sir Robert Harcliffe and Sir William,
　　Sir James, that bold barron.

And with Sir George and Sir James,
　　Both knights of good account,
Good Sir Raphe Rebbye there was slaine,
　　Whose prowesse did surmount.

For Witherington needs must I wayle
　　As one in dolefull dumpes,
For when his leggs were smitten of,
　　He fought upon his stumpes.

And with Erle Dowglas there was slaine
  Sir Hugh Mountgomerye,
And Sir Charles Morrell, that from feelde
  One foote wold never flee;

Sir Roger Hever of Harcliffe tow,
  His sisters sonne was hee;
Sir David Lambwell, well esteemed,
  But saved he cold not bee.

And the Lord Maxwell, in like case,
  With Douglas he did dye;
Of twenty hundred Scottish speeres,
  Scarce fifty-five did flye.

Of fifteen hundred Englishmen
  Went home but fifty-three;
The rest in Chevy Chase were slaine,
  Under the greenwoode tree.

Next day did many widdowes come
  Their husbands to bewayle;
They washt their wounds in brinish teares,
  But all wold not prevayle.

Theyr bodyes, bathed in purple blood,
  They bore with them away;
They kist them dead a thousand times
  Ere they were cladd in clay.

The newes was brought to Eddenborrow,
  Where Scottlands king did rayne,
That brave Erle Douglas soddainlye
  Was with an arrow slaine.

'O heavy newes!' King James can say;
    'Scottland may wittenesse bee
I have not any captaine more
    Of such account as hee.'

Like tydings to King Henery came,
    Within as short a space,
That Pearcy of Northumberland
    Was slaine in Chevy Chase.

'Now God be with him!' said our king,
    'Sith it will noe better bee;
I trust I have within my realme
    Five hundred as good as hee.

'Yett shall not Scotts nor Scotland say
    But I will vengeance take,
And be revenged on them all
    For brave Erle Percyes sake.'

This vow the king did well performe
    After on Humble-downe;
In one day fifty knights were slayne,
    With lords of great renowne.

And of the rest of small account,
    Did many hundreds dye:
Thus endeth the hunting in Chevy Chase,
    Made by the Erle Pearcye.

God save our king, and blesse this land
    With plentye, ioy, and peace,
And grant hencforth that foule debate
    Twixt noble men may ceaze!

Johnie Armstrong

There dwelt a man in faire Westmerland,
  Jonnë Armestrong men did him call,
He had nither lands nor rents coming in,
  Yet he kept eight score men in his hall.

He had horse and harness for them all,
  Goodly steeds were all milke-white;
O the golden bands an about their necks,
  And their weapons, they were all alike.

Newes then was brought unto the king
  That there was a sicke a won as hee,
That livëd lyke a bold out-law,
  And robbëd all the north country.

The king he writt an a letter then,
  A letter which was large and long;
He signëd it with his owne hand,
  And he promised to doe him no wrong.

When this letter came Jonnë untill,
  His heart it was as blythe as birds on the tree:
'Never was I sent for before any king,
  My father, my grandfather, nor none but mee.

'And if wee goe the king before,
  I would we went most orderly;
Every man of you shall have his scarlet cloak,
  Laced with silver laces three.

'Every won of you shall have his velvett coat,
  Laced with silver lace so white;

O the golden bands an about your necks,
    Black hatts, white feathers, all alyke.'

By the morrow morninge at ten of the clock,
    Towards Edenburough gon was hee,
And with him all his eight score men;
    Good lord, it was a goodly sight for to see!

When Jonnë came befower the king,
    He fell downe on his knee;
'O pardon, my soveraine leige,' he said,
    'O pardon my eight score men and mee!'

'Thou shalt have no pardon, thou traytor strong,
    For thy eight score men nor thee;
For to-morrow morning by ten of the clock,
    Both thou and them shall hang on the gallow-tree.'

But Jonnë looke'd over his left shoulder,
    Good Lord, what a grevious look looked hee!
Saying, 'Asking grace of a graceless face—
    Why there is none for you nor me.'

But Jonnë had a bright sword by his side,
    And it was made of the mettle so free,
That had not the king stept his foot aside,
    He had smitten his head from his faire boddë.

Saying, 'Fight on, my merry men all,
    And see that none of you be taine;
For rather then men shall say we were hange'd,
    Let them report how we were slaine.'

Then, God wott, faire Eddenburrough rose,
    And so besett poore Jonnë rounde,
That fowerscore and tenn of Jonnës best men
    Lay gasping all upon the ground.

Then like a mad man Jonnë laide about,
    And like a mad man then fought hee,
Untill a falce Scot came Jonnë behinde,
    And runn him through the faire boddee.

Saying, 'Fight on, my merry men all,
    And see that none of you be taine;
For I will stand by and bleed but awhile,
    And then will I come and fight againe.'

Newes then was brought to young Jonnë Armestrong,
    As he stood by his nurses knee,
Who vowed if ere he live'd for to be a man,
    O the treacherous Scots revengd hee'd be.

Johnie Cock

Johny he has risen up i' the morn,
    Calls for water to wash his hands;
But little knew he that his bloody hounds
    Were bound in iron bands, bands,
    Were bound in iron bands.

Johny's mother has gotten word o' that,
    And care-bed she has tane:
'O Johny, for my benison,
    I beg you'l stay at hame;
For the wine so red, and the well baken bread,
    My Johny shall want nane.

'There are seven forsters at Pickeram Side,
    At Pickeram where they dwell,
And for a drop of thy heart's bluid
    They wad ride the fords of hell.'

Johny he's gotten word of that,
    And he's turn'd wondrous keen;
He's put off the red scarlett,
    And he's put on the Lincolm green.

With a sheaf of arrows by his side,
    And a bent bow in his hand,
He's mounted on a prancing steed,
    And he has ridden fast o'er the strand.

He's up i' Braidhouplee, and down i' Bradyslee,
    And up under a buss o broom,
And there he found a good dun deer,
    Feeding in a buss of ling.

Johny shot, and the dun deer lap,
    And she lap wondrous wide,
Until they came to the wan water,
    And he stemd her out of her pride.

He 'as taen out the little pen-knife,
    'Twas full three quarters long,
And he has ta'en out of that dun deer
    The liver bot and the tongue.

They eat of the flesh, and they drank of the blood,
    And the blood it was so sweet,
Which caused Johny and his bloody hounds
    To fall in a deep sleep.

By then came an old palmer,
    And an ill death may he die!
For he's away to Pickram Side,
    As fast as he can drie.

'What news, what news?' says the Seven Forsters,
   'What news have ye brought to me?'
'I have noe news,' the palmer said,
   'But what I saw with my eye.

'High up i' Bradyslee, low down i' Bradisslee,
   And under a buss of scroggs,
O there I spied a well-wight man,
   Sleeping among his dogs.

'His coat it was of light Lincolm,
   And his breeches of the same,
His shoes of the American leather,
   And gold buckles tying them.'

Up bespake the Seven Forsters,
   Up bespake they ane and a':
O that is Johny o Cockley's Well,
   And near him we will draw.

O the first y stroke that they gae him,
   They struck him off by the knee;
Then up bespake his sister's son:
   'O the next'll gar him die!'

'O some they count ye well-wight men,
   But I do count ye nane;
For you might well ha waken'd me,
   And askd gin I wad be taen.

'The wildest wolf in aw this wood
   Wad not ha done so by me;
She'd ha wet her foot ith wan water,
   And sprinkled it oer my brae,
And if that wad not ha waken'd me,
   She wad ha gone and let me be.

'O bows of yew, if ye be true,
   In London where ye were bought,
Fingers five, get up belive,
   Manhuid shall fail me nought.'

He has kill'd the Seven Forsters,
   He has kill'd them all but ane,
And that wan scarce to Pickeram Side,
   To carry the bode-words hame.

'Is there never a boy in a' this wood
   That will tell what I can say;
That will go to Cockley's Well,
   Tell my mither to fetch me away?'

There was a boy into that wood,
   That carried the tidings away,
And many ae was the well-wight man
   At the fetching o Johny away.

Captain Car
(*Edom o' Gordon*)

It fell about the Martinmas,
   When the wind blew schrile and cauld,
Said Edom o Gordon to his men,
   'We maun draw to a hald.

'And what an a hald sall we draw to,
   My merry men and me?
We will gae to the house of the Rhodes,
   To see that fair lady.'

She had nae sooner busket hersell,
   Nor putten on her gown,
Till Edom o Gordon and his men
   Were round about the town.

They had nae sooner sitten down,
   Nor sooner said the grace,
Till Edom o Gordon and his men
   Were closed about the place.

The lady ran up to her tower-head,
   As fast as she could drie,
To see if by her fair speeches
   She could with him agree.

As soon as he saw the lady fair,
   And hir yates all locked fast,
He fell into a rage of wrath,
   And his heart was aghast.

'Cum down to me, ye lady fair,
   Cum down to me; let's see;
This night ye's ly by my ain side,
   The morn my bride sall be.'

'I winnae cum down, ye fals Gordon,
   I winnae cum down to thee;
I winnae forsake my ane dear lord,
   That is sae far frae me.'

'Gi' up your house, ye fair lady,
   Gi' up your house to me,
Or I will burn yoursel therein,
   Bot and your babies three.'

'I winnae gie up, you fals Gordon,
    To nae sik traitor as thee,
Tho you should burn mysel therein,
    Bot and babies three.'

'Set fire to the house,' quoth fals Gordon,
    'Sin better may nae bee;
And I will burn hersel therein,
    Bot and her babies three.'

'And ein wae worth ye, Jock my man!
    I paid ye weil your fee;
Why pow ye out my ground-wa-stane,
    Lets in the reek to me?

'And ein wae worth ye, Jock my man!
    For I paid you weil your hire;
Why pow ye out my ground-wa-stane,
    To me lets in the fire?'

'Ye paid me weil my hire, lady,
    Ye paid me weil my fee,
But now I'm Edom o Gordon's man,
    Maun either do or die.'

O then bespake her youngest son,
    Sat on the nurse's knee,
'Dear mother, gi'e owre your house,' he says,
    'For the reek it worries me.'

'I winnae gi'e up my house, my dear,
    To nae sik traitor as he;
Cum weil, cum wae, my jewels fair,
    Ye maun tak share wi me.'

O then bespake her dochter dear,
    She was baith jimp and sma;
'O row me in a pair o shiets,
    And tow me owre the wa.'

They rowd her in a pair of shiets,
    And towd her owre the wa,
But on the point of Edom's speir
    She gat a deadly fa.

O bonny, bonny was hir mouth,
    And chirry were her cheiks,
And clear, clear was hir yellow hair,
    Where on the red bluid dreips!

Then wi his speir he turnd hir owr;
    O gin hir face was wan!
He said, 'You are the first that eer
    I wist alive again.'

He turnd hir owr and owr again;
    O gin hir skin was whyte!
He said, 'I might ha spard thy life
    To been some man's delyte.'

'Busk and boon, my merry men all,
    For ill dooms I do guess;
I cannae luik in that bonny face,
    As it lyes on the grass.'

'Them luiks to freits, my master deir,
    Then freits will follow them;
Let it neir be said brave Edom o Gordon
    Was daunted with a dame.'

O then he spied hir ain dear lord,
    As he came owr the lee;
He saw his castle in a fire,
    As far as he could see.

'Put on, put on, my mighty men,
    As fast as ye can drie!
For he that's hindmost of my men
    Sall neir get guid of me.'

And some they raid, and some they ran,
    Fu fast out-owr the plain,
But lang, lang eer he coud get up
    They were a' deid and slain.

But mony were the mudie men
    Lay gasping on the grien;
For o fifty men that Edom brought out
    There were but five ged heme.

And mony were the mudie men
    Lay gasping on the grien,
And mony were the fair ladys
    Lay lemanless at heme.

And round and round the waes he went,
    Their ashes for to view;
At last into the flames he flew,
    And bad the world adieu.

III

Scots Eighteenth Century

Edward

'Why dois your brand sae drap wi bluid,
        Edward, Edward,
Why dois your brand sae drap wi bluid,
   And why sae sad gang yee O ?'
'O I hae killed my hauke sae guid,
        Mither, mither,
O I hae killed my hauke sae guid,
   And I had nae mair bot hee O.'

'Your haukis bluid was nevir sae reid,
        Edward, Edward,
Your haukis bluid was nevir sae reid,
   My deir son I tell thee O.'
'O I hae killed my reid-roan steid,
        Mither, mither,
O I hae killed my reid-roan steid,
   That erst was sae fair and frie O.'

'Your steid was auld, and ye hae gat mair,
        Edward, Edward,
Your steid was auld, and ye hae gat mair,
   Sum other dule ye drie O.'
'O I hae killed my fadir deir,
        Mither, mither,
O I hae killed my fadir deir,
   Alas, and wae is mee O!'

'And whatten penance wul ye drie for that,
        Edward, Edward ?
And whatten penance will ye drie for that ?
   My deir son, now tell me O.'

'Ile set my feit in yonder boat,
   Mither, mither,
Ile set my feit in yonder boat,
 And Ile fare ovir the sea O.'

'And what wul ye doe wi your towirs and your ha,
   Edward, Edward?
And what wul ye doe wi your towirs and your ha,
 That were sae fair to see O?'
'Ile let thame stand tul they doun fa,
   Mither, mither,
Ile let thame stand tul they doun fa,
 For here nevir mair maun I bee O.'

'And what wul ye leive to your bairns and your wife,
   Edward, Edward?
And what wul ye leive to your bairns and your wife,
 Whan ye gang ovir the sea O?'
'The warldis room, late them beg thrae life,
   Mither, mither,
The warldis room, late them beg thrae life,
 For thame nevir mair wul I see O.'

'And what wul ye leive to your ain mither deir,
   Edward, Edward?
And what wul ye leive to your ain mither deir?
 My deir son, now tell me O.'
'The curse of hell frae me sall ye beir,
   Mither, mither,
The curse of hell frae me sall ye beir,
 Sic counseils ye gave to me O.'

Sir Patrick Spens

The king sits in Dumferling toune,
   Drinking the blude-reid wine:
'O whar will I get guid sailor,
   To sail this schip of mine?'

Up and spak an eldern knicht,
   Sat at the kings richt kne:
'Sir Patrick Spence is the best sailor
   That sails upon the se.'

The king has written a braid letter,
   And signed wi' his hand,
And sent it to Sir Patrick Spence,
   Was walking on the sand.

The first line that Sir Patrick red,
   A loud lauch lauched he;
The next line that Sir Patrick red,
   The teir blinded his ee.

'O wha is this has done this deid,
   This ill deid don to me,
To send me out this time o' the yeir,
   To sail upon the se?'

'Mak hast, mak hast, my mirry men all,
   Our guid schip sails the morne:'
'O say na sae, my master deir,
   For I feir a deadlie storme.'

'Late late yestreen I saw the new moone,
  Wi' the auld moone in hir arme,
And I feir, I feir, my deir master,
  That we will cum to harme.'

O our Scots nobles were rich laith
  To weet their cork-heild schoone;
Bot lang owre a' the play wer playd,
  Thair hats they swam aboone.

O lang, lang, may their ladies sit,
  Wi' thair fans into their hand,
Or eir they se Sir Patrick Spence
  Cum sailing to the land.

O lang, lang, may the ladies stand,
  Wi' thair gold kems in their hair,
Waiting for their ain deir lords,
  For they'll se thame na mair.

Have owre, have owre to Aberdour,
  It's fifty fadom deip,
And thair lies guid Sir Patrick Spence,
  Wi' the Scots lords at his feit.

Lord Thomas and Fair Annet

Lord Thomas and fair Annet
  Sate a' the day on a hill;
Whan night was cum, and sun was sett,
  They had not talkt their fill.

Lord Thomas said a word in jest,
  Fair Annet took it ill:
'A, I will nevir wed a wife
  Against my ain friends' will.'

'Gif ye wull nevir wed a wife,
    A wife wull neir wed yee.'
Sae he is hame to tell his mither,
    And knelt upon his knee.

'O rede, O rede, mither,' he says,
    'A gude rede gie to mee;
O sall I tak the nut-browne bride,
    And let fair Annet bee?'

'The nut-browne bride has gowd and gear,
    Fair Annet she has gat nane;
And the little beauty fair Annet haes
    O it wull soon be gane.'

And he has till his brother gane:
    'Now, brother, rede ye mee;
A, sall I marrie the nut-browne bride,
    And let fair Annet bee?'

'The nut-browne bride has oxen, brother,
    The nut-browne bride has kye;
I wad hae ye marrie the nut-browne bride,
    And cast fair Annet bye.'

'Her oxen may dye i' the house, billie,
    And her kye into the byre,
And I sall hae nothing to mysell
    Bot a fat fadge by the fyre.'

And he has till his sister gane:
    'Now, sister, rede ye mee;
O sall I marrie the nut-browne bride,
    And set fair Annet free?'

'I'se rede ye tak fair Annet, Thomas,
    And let the browne bride alane;
Lest ye sould sigh and say, Alace!
    What is this we brought hame?'

'No, I will tak my mither's counsel,
    And marrie me owt o' hand;
And I will tak the nut-browne bride,
    Fair Annet may leive the land.'

Up then rose fair Annet's father,
    Twa hours or it were day.
And he is gane into the bower
    Wherein fair Annet lay.

'Rise up, rise up, fair Annet,' he says,
    'Put on your silken sheene;
Let us gae to St. Marie's kirke,
    And see that rich weddeen.'

'My maides, gae to my dressing-room,
    And dress to me my hair;
Whair-eir yee laid a plait before,
    See yee lay ten times mair.

'My maides, gae to my dressing-room,
    And dress to me my smock;
The one half is o' the holland fine,
    The other o' needle-work.'

The horse fair Annet rade upon,
    He amblit like the wind;
Wi' siller he was shod before,
    Wi' burning gowd behind.

Four and twenty siller bells
    Wer a' tyed till his mane,
And yae tift o' the norland winde,
    They tinkled ane by ane.

Four and twenty gay gude knichts
    Rade by fair Annet's side,
And four and twenty fair ladies,
    As gin she had bin a bride.

And whan she cam to Marie's kirk,
    She sat on Marie's stean:
The cleading that fair Annet had on
    It skinkled in their een.

And whan she cam into the kirk,
    She shimmerd like the sun;
The belt that was about her waist
    Was a' wi pearles bedone.

She sat her by the nut-browne bride,
    And her een they wer sae clear,
Lord Thomas he clean forgat the bride,
    When fair Annet drew near.

He had a rose into his hand,
    He gae it kisses three,
And reaching by the nut-browne bride,
    Laid it on fair Annet's knee.

Up than spak the nut-browne bride,
    She spak wi' meikle spite:
'And whair gat ye that rose-water,
    That does mak yee sae white?'

'O I did get the rose-water
  Whair ye wull neir get nane,
For I did get that very rose-water
  Into my mither's wame.'

The bride she drew a long bodkin
  Frae out her gay head gear,
And strake fair Annet unto the heart,
  That word spak nevir mair.

Lord Thomas he saw fair Annet wex pale,
  And marvelit what mote bee;
But whan he saw her dear heart's blude,
  A' wood-wroth wexed hee.

He drew his dagger, that was sae sharp,
  That was sae sharp and meet,
And drave it into the nut-browne bride,
  That fell deid at his feit.

'Now stay for me, dear Annet,' he sed,
  'Now stay, my dear,' he cry'd;
Then strake the dagger untill his heart,
  And fell deid by her side.

Lord Thomas was buried without kirk-wa,
  Fair Annet within the quiere,
And o' the tane thair grew a birk,
  The other a bonny briere.

And ay they grew, and ay they threw,
  As they wad faine be neare;
And by this ye may ken right weil
  They were twa luvers deare.

Thomas Rymer

True Thomas lay o'er yond grass bank,
   And he beheld a lady gay,
A lady that was brisk and bold,
   Come riding o'er the fernie brae.

Her skirt was of the grass-green silk,
   Her mantel of the velvet fine,
At ilka tate o' her horse's mane,
   Hung fifty siller bells and nine.

True Thomas he took off his hat,
   And bowed him low down till his knee:
'All hail, thou mighty Queen of Heaven!
   For your like on earth I never did see.'

'O no, O no, True Thomas,' she says,
   'That name does not belong to me;
I am but the queen of fair Elfland,
   And I am come here for to visit thee.

'But ye maun go wi' me now, Thomas,
   True Thomas, ye maun go wi' me,
Foe ye maun serve me seven years,
   Thro weel or wae as may chance to be.'

She turned about her milk-white steed,
   And took True Thomas up behind,
And aye whene'er bridle rang,
   The steed flew swifter than the wind.

For forty days and forty nights,
    He wade thro red blude to the knee,
And he saw neither sun nor moon,
    But heard the roaring of the sea.

O they rade on, and farther on,
    Until they came to a garden green:
'Light down, light down, ye ladie free,
    Some of that fruit let me pull to thee.'

'O no, O no, True Thomas,' she says,
    'That fruit maun not be touched by thee,
For a' the plagues that are in hell
    Light on the fruit of this countrie.

'But I have a loaf here in my lap,
    Likewise a bottle of claret wine,
And now ere we go farther on,
    We'll rest a while, and ye may dine.'

When he had eaten and drunk his fill,
    'Lay down your head upon my knee,'
The lady sayd, 'ere we climb yon hill,
    And I will show you ferlies three.

'O see not ye yon narrow road,
    So thick beset wi' thorns and briers?
That is the path of righteousness,
    Tho after it but few enquires.

'And see not ye yon braid braid road,
    That lies across yon lilly leven?
That is the path of wickedness,
    Tho some call it the road to heaven.

'And see not ye that bonny road,
  Which winds about the fernie brae?
That is the road to fair Elfland,
  Where you and I this night maun gae.

'But Thomas, ye maun hold your tongue,
  Whatever you may hear or see,
For gin ae word you should chance to speak,
  You will neer get back to your ain countrie.'

He has gotten a coat of the even cloth,
  And a pair of shoes of velvet green,
And till seven years were past and gone
  True Thomas on earth was never seen.

Tam Lin

O I forbid you, maidens a',
  That wear gowd on your hair,
To come or gae by Carterhaugh,
  For young Tam Lin is there.

There's nane that gaes by Carterhaugh,
  But they leave him a wad,
Either their rings, or green mantles,
  Or else their maidenhead.

Janet has kilted her green kirtle
  A little aboon her knee,
And she has broded her yellow hair
  A little aboon her bree,
And she's awa to Carterhaugh,
  As fast as she can hie.

When she came to Carterhaugh
   Tam Lin was at the well,
And there she fand his steed standing,
   But away was himsel.

She had na pu'd a double rose,
   A rose but only twa,
Till up then started young Tam Lin,
   Says, 'Lady, thou pu's nae mae.

'Why pu's thou the rose, Janet,
   And why breaks thou the wand?
Or why comes thou to Carterhaugh
   Withoutten my command?'

'Carterhaugh, it is my ain,
   My daddie gave it me;
I'll come and gang by Carterhaugh,
   And ask nae leave at thee.'

Janet has kilted her green kirtle
   A little aboon her knee,
And she has snooded her yellow hair
   A little aboon her bree,
And she is to her father's ha',
   As fast as she can hie.

Four and twenty ladies fair
   Were playing at the ba',
And out then cam the fair Janet,
   Ance the flower among them a'.

Four and twenty ladies fair
   Were playing at the chess,
And out then cam the fair Janet,
   As green as onie glass.

Out then spak an auld grey knight,
    Lay o'er the castle wa',
And says, 'Alas, fair Janet, for thee
    But we'll be blamed a'.'

'Haud your tongue, ye auld fac'd knight,
    Some ill death may ye die!
Father my bairn on whom I will,
    I'll father nane on thee.'

Out then spak her father dear,
    And he spak meek and mild:
'And ever alas, sweet Janet,' he says,
    'I think thou gaes wi' child.'

'If that I gae wi' child, father,
    Mysel maun bear the blame;
There's neer a laird about your ha'
    Shall get the bairn's name.

'If my love were an earthly knight,
    As he's an elfin grey,
I wad na gie my ain true-love
    For nae lord that ye hae.

'The steed that my true-love rides on
    Is lighter than the wind;
Wi' siller he is shod before,
    Wi' burning gowd behind.'

Janet has kilted her green kirtle
    A little aboon her knee,
And she has snooded her yellow hair
    A little aboon her bree,
And she's awa to Carterhaugh,
    As fast as she can hie.

When she cam to Carterhaugh,
    Tam Lin was at the well,
And there she fand his steed standing,
    But away was himsel.

She had na pu'd a double rose,
    A rose but only twa,
Till up then started young Tam Lin,
    Says, 'Lady, thou pu's nae mae.'

'Why pu's thou the rose, Janet,
    Amang the groves saw green,
And a' to kill the bonnie babe,
    That we gat us between?'

'O tell me, tell me, Tam Lin,' she says,
    'For's sake that died on tree,
If eer ye was in holy chapel,
    Or christendom did see?'

'Roxbrugh he was my grandfather,
    Took me with him to bide,
And ance it fell upon a day
    That wae did me betide.

'And ance it fell upon a day,
    A cauld day and a snell,
When we were frae the hunting come,
    That frae my horse I fell;
The Queen o Fairies she caught me,
    In yon green hill to dwell.

'And pleasant is the fairy land,
    But, an eerie tale to tell,
Ay at the end of seven years
    We pay a tiend to hell;

I am sae fair and fu o flesh,
    I'm feard it be mysel.

'But the night is Halloween, lady,
    The morn is Hallowday;
Then win me, win me, an ye will,
    For weel I wat ye may.

'Just at the mirk and midnight hour
    The fairy folk will ride,
And they that wad their tru-love win,
    At Miles Cross they maun bide.'

'But how shall I thee ken, Tam Lin,
    Or how my true-love know,
Amang sae mony unco knights
    The like I never saw?'

'O first let pass the black, lady,
    And syne let pass the brown,
But quickly run to the milk-white steed,
    Pu ye his rider down.

'For I'll ride on the milk-white steed,
    And ay nearest the town;
Because I was an earthly knight
    They gie me that renown.

'My right hand will be glovd, lady,
    My left hand will be bare,
Cockt up shall my bonnet be,
    And kaimd down shall my hair,
And thae's the takens I gie thee,
    Nae doubt I will be there.

'They'll turn me in your arms, lady,
  Into an esk and adder;
But hold me fast, and fear me not,
  I am your bairn's father.

'They'll turn me to a bear sae grim,
  And then a lion bold;
But hold me fast, and fear me not,
  As ye shall love your child.

'Again they'll turn me in your arms
  To a red hot gaud of airn;
But hold me fast, and fear me not,
  I'll do to you nae harm.

'And last they'll turn me in your arms
  Into the burning gleed;
Then throw me into well water,
  O throw me in wi' speed.

'And then I'll be your ain true-love,
  I'll turn a naked knight;
Then cover me wi' your green mantle,
  And cover me out o sight.'

Gloomy, gloomy was the night,
  And eerie was the way,
As fair Jenny in her green mantle
  To Miles Cross she did gae.

About the middle o the night
  She heard the bridles ring;
This lady was as glad at that
  As any earthly thing.

134

First she let the black pass by,
  And syne she let the brown;
But quickly she ran to the milk-white steed,
  And pu'd the rider down.

Sae weel she minded what he did say,
  And young Tam Lin did win;
Syne coverd him wi' her green mantle,
  As blythe's a bird in spring.

Out then spak the Queen o Fairies,
  Out of a bush o broom:
'Them that has gotten young Tam Lin
  Has gotten a stately groom.'

Out then spak the Queen o Fairies,
  And an angry woman was she:
'Shame betide her ill-far'd face,
  And an ill death may she die,
For she's taen awa the bonniest knight
  In a' my companie.

'But had I kend, Tam Lin,' she says,
  'What now this night I see,
I wad hae taen out thy twa grey een,
  And put in twa een o tree.'

Geordie

There was a battle in the north,
  And nobles there was many,
And they hae killd Sir Charlie Hay,
  And they laid the wyte on Geordie.

O he has written a lang letter,
    He sent it to his lady:
'Ye maun come up to Enbrugh town,
    To see what word's o Geordie.'

When she first lookd the letter on,
    She was baith red and rosy;
But she had na read a word but twa
    Till she wallowt like a lily.

'Gar get to me my gude grey steed,
    My menyie a' gae wi me,
For I shall neither eat nor drink
    Till Enbrugh town shall see me.'

And she has mountit her gude grey steed,
    Her menyie a' gaed wi her,
And she did neither eat nor drink
    Till Enbrugh town did see her.

And first appeard the fatal block,
    And syne the aix to head him,
And Geordie cumin down the stair,
    And bands o airn upon him.

But tho he was chaind in fetters strang,
    O airn and steel sae heavy,
There was na ane in a' the court
    Sae bra a man as Geordie.

O she's down on her bended knee,
    I wat she's pale and weary:
'O pardon, pardon, noble king,
    And gie me back my dearie!

'I hae born seven sons to my Geordie dear,
     The seventh neer saw his daddie;
O pardon, pardon, noble king,
     Pity a waeful lady!'

'Gar bid the headin-man mak haste,'
     Our king reply'd fu lordly:
'O noble king, tak a' that's mine,
     But gie me back my Geordie!'

The Gordons cam, and the Gordons ran,
     And they were stark and steady,
And ay the word amang them a'
     Was, Gordons, keep you ready!

An aged lord at the king's right hand
     Says, Noble king, but hear me;
Gar her tell down five thousand pound,
     And gie her back her dearie.

Some gae her marks, some gae her crowns,
     Some gae her dollars many,
And she's telld down five thousand pound,
     And she's gotten again her dearie.

She blinkit blythe in her Geordie's face,
     Says, Dear I've bought thee, Geordie;
But there sud been bluidy bouks on the green
     Or I had tint my laddie.

He claspit her by the middle sma,
     And he kist her lips sae rosy:
'The fairest flower o' woman-kind
     Is my sweet, bonie lady!'

Mary Hamilton

Word's gane to the kitchen,
　　And word's gane to the ha,
That Marie Hamilton gangs wi bairn
　　To the hichest Stewart of a'.

He's courted her in the kitchen,
　　He's courted her in the ha,
He's courted her in the laigh cellar,
　　And that was warst of a'.

She's tyed it in her apron
　　And she's thrown it in the sea;
Says, 'Sink ye, swim ye, bonny wee babe!
　　You'l neer get mair o me.'

Down then cam the auld queen,
　　Goud tassels tying her hair:
'O Marie, where's the bonny wee babe
　　That I heard greet sae sair?'

'There never was a babe intill my room,
　　As little designs to be;
It was but a touch o my sair side,
　　Come oer my fair bodie.'

'O Marie, put on your robes o black,
　　Or else your robes o brown,
For ye maun gang wi me the night,
　　To see fair Edinbro town.'

'I winna put on my robes o black,
  Nor yet my robes o brown;
But I'll put on my robes o white,
  To shine through Edinbro town.'

When she gaed up the Cannogate,
  She laughd loud laughters three;
But whan she cam down the Cannogate
  The tear blinded her ee.

When she gaed up the Parliament stair,
  The heel cam aff her shee;
And lang or she cam down again
  She was condemnd to dee.

When she cam down the Cannogate,
  The Cannogate sae free,
Many a ladie lookd oer her window,
  Weeping for this ladie.

'Ye need nae weep for me,' she says,
  'Ye need nae weep for me;
For had I not slain mine own sweet babe,
  This death I wadna dee.

'Bring me a bottle of wine,' she says,
  'The best that eer ye hae,
That I may drink to my weil-wishers,
  And they may drink to me.

'Here's a health to the jolly sailors,
  That sail upon the main;
Let them never let on to my father and mother
  But what I'm coming hame.

'Here's a health to the jolly sailors,
    That sail upon the sea;
Let them never let on to my father and mother
    That I cam here to dee.

'Oh little did my mother think,
    The day she cradled me,
What lands I was to travel through,
    What death I was to dee.

'Oh little did my father think,
    The day he held up me,
What lands I was to travel through,
    What death I was to dee.

'Last night I washd the queen's feet,
    And gently laid her down;
And a' the thanks I've gotten the nicht
    To be hangd in Edinbro town!

'Last nicht there was four Maries,
    The nicht there'l be but three;
There was Marie Seton, and Marie Beton,
    And Marie Carmichael, and me.'

IV

Folksong and Lyric

FOLKSONG AND LYRIC

O Waly, Waly

(*Jamie Douglas*)

O waly, waly up the bank!
   And waly, waly, down the brae!
And waly, waly yon burn-side,
   Where I and my love wont to gae!

I lean'd my back unto an aik,
   I thought it was a trusty tree;
But first it bow'd, and syne it brak,
   Sae my true love did lightly me.

O waly, waly! but love be bonny
   A little time, while it is new;
But when 'tis auld, it waxeth cauld,
   And fades away like morning dew.

O wherefore shou'd I busk my head?
   Or wherefore shou'd I kame my hair?
For my true-love has me forsook,
   And says he'll never love me mair.

Now Arthur-Seat shall be my bed,
   The sheets shall neer be fyl'd by me;
Saint Anton's well shall be my drink,
   Since my true-love has forsaken me.

Martinmas wind, when wilt thou blaw,
   And shake the green leaves off the tree?
O gentle death, when wilt thou come?
   For of my life I am weary.

'Tis not the frost that freezes fell,
   Nor blawing snaw's inclemency;

143

'Tis not sic cauld that makes me cry,
 But my love's heart grown cauld to me.

When we came in by Glasgow town,
 We were a comely sight to see;
My love was cled in the black velvet,
 And I my sell in cramasie.

But had I wist, before I kiss'd,
 That love had been sae ill to win,
I'd locked my heart in a case of gold,
 And pin'd it with a silver pin.

Oh, oh, if my young babes were born,
 And set upon the nurse's knee,
And I my sell were dead and gane!
 For a maid again I'll never be.

The Bonny Earl of Murray

Ye Highlands, and ye Lawlands,
 Oh where have you been?
They have slain the Earl of Murray,
 And they layd him on the green.

'Now wae be to thee, Huntly!
 And wherefore did you sae?
I bade you bring him wi you,
 But forbade you him to slay.'

He was a braw gallant,
 And he rid at the ring;
And the bonny Earl of Murray,
 Oh he might have been a king!

He was a braw gallant,
   And he played at the ba;
And the bonny Earl of Murray
   Was the flower amang them a'.

He was a braw gallant,
   And played at the glove;
And the bonny Earl of Murray,
   Oh he was the Queen's love!

Oh lang will his lady
   Look oer the castle Down,
Eer she see the Earl of Murray
   Come sounding thro the town!

Bonnie George Campbell

Hie upon Hielands,
   and laigh upon Tay,
Bonnie George Campbell
   rode out on a day.

He saddled, he bridled,
   and gallant rode he,
And hame cam his guid horse,
   but never cam he.

Out cam his mother dear,
   greeting fu sair,
And out cam his bonnie bryde,
   riving her hair.

'The meadow lies green,
   the corn is unshorn,
But bonnie George Campbell
   will never return.'

Saddled and bridled
    and booted rode he,
A plume in his helmet,
    A sword at his knee.

But toom cam his saddle,
    all bloody to see,
Oh, hame cam his guid horse,
    but never cam he!

The Unquiet Grave

Cold blows the wind to my true love,
    And gently drops the rain,
I never had but one sweetheart,
    And in greenwood she lies slain,
    And in greenwood she lies slain.

I'll do as much for my sweetheart
    As any young man may;
I'll sit and mourn all on her grave
    For a twelvemonth and a day.

When the twelvemonth and one day was past,
    The ghost began to speak;
'Why sittest here all on my grave,
    And will not let me sleep?'

'There's one thing that I want, sweetheart,
    There's one thing that I crave;
And that is a kiss from your lily-white lips—
    Then I'll go from your grave.'

'My breast it is as cold as clay,
  My breath smells earthly strong;
And if you kiss my cold clay lips,
  Your days they won't be long.

'Go fetch me water from the desert,
  And blood from out of a stone;
Go fetch me milk from a fair maid's breast
  That a young man never had known.'

'O down in yonder grove, sweetheart,
  Where you and I would walk,
The first flower that ever I saw
  Is withered to a stalk.

'The stalk is wither'd and dry, sweetheart,
  And the flower will never return;
And since I lost my own sweetheart,
  What can I do but mourn?

'When shall we meet again, sweetheart?
  When shall we meet again?'
'When the oaken leaves that fall from the trees
  Are green and spring up again,
  Are green and spring up again.'

Still Growing

The trees they do grow high, and the leaves they do grow green;
  The time is gone and past, my love, that you and I have seen:
It's a cold winter's night, my love, when you and I must bide
    alone,
  The bonny lad was young,
    But a-growing.

'O father, dear father, I'm feared you've done me harm,
  You've married me to a boy and I fear he is too young.'
'O daughter, dear daughter, and if you stay at home and wait
      along o' me
  A lady you shall be,
    While he's a-growing.

'We'll send him to the college for one year or two
  And then perhaps in time, my love, a man he will grow,
I will buy you a bunch of white ribbons to tie about his bonny,
      bonny waist
  To let the ladies know
    That he's married.'

At the age of sixteen, he was a married man,
  At the age of seventeen, he brought him a son;
At the age of eighteen, my love, O his grave was growing green,
  And so she put an end
    To his growing.

'I made my love a shroud of the holland so fine,'
  And every stitch she put in it the tears came trickling down;
O once I had a sweetheart, but now I have got never a one,
  So fare you well my own true love
    For ever.

The Grey Cock

All on one summer's evening when the fever were a-dawning
I heard a fair maid make a mourn.
She was a-weeping for her father and a-grieving for her mother,
And a-thinking all on her true love John.
At last Johnny came and he found the doors all shut,
And he dingled so low at the ring.
Then this fair maid she rose and she hurried on her clothes
To make haste to let Johnny come in.

All around the waist he caught her and unto the bed he brought
    her,
And they lay there a-talking awhile.
She says: O you feathered fowls, you pretty feathered fowls,
Don't you crow till 'tis almost day,
And your comb it shall be of the pure ivory
And your wings of the bright silveree.
But him a-being young, he crowed very soon,
He crowed two long hours before day;
And she sent her love away, for she thought 'twas almost day.
And 'twas all by the light of the moon.

It's when will you be back, dear Johnny,
When will you be back to see me?
When the seventh moon is done and passed and shines on
    yonder lea,
And you know that will never be.
What a foolish girl was I when I thought he was as true
As the rocks that grow to the ground;
But since I do find he has altered his mind,
It's better to live single than bound.

The Streams of Lovely Nancy

Oh, the streams of lovely Nancy are divided in three parts,
Where the young men and maidens they do meet their
    sweethearts.
It is drinking of good liquor caused my heart for to sing,
And the noise in yonder village made the rocks for to ring.

At the top of this mountain, there my love's castle stands.
It's all overbuilt with ivory on yonder black sand,
Fine arches, fine porches, and diamonds so bright.
It's a pilot for a sailor on a dark winter's night.

On yonder high mountain, where the wild fowl do fly,
There is one amongst them that flies very high.
If I had her in my arms, love, near the diamond's black land,
How soon I'd secure her by the sleight of my hand.

At the bottom of the mountain there runs a river clear.
A ship from the Indies did once anchor there,
With her red flags a-flying and the beating of her drum,
Sweet instruments of music and the firing of her gun.

So come all you little streamers that walk the meadows gay,
I'll write unto my true love, wherever she may be,
For her rosy lips entice me, with her tongue she tells me 'No',
And an angel might direct us right, and where shall we go?

Six Dukes went a-Fishing

Six dukes went a-fishing
Down by yon sea-side.
One of them spied a dead body
Lain by the waterside.

The one said to the other,
These words I heard them say:
'It's the Royal Duke of Grantham
That the tide has washed away.'

They took him up to Portsmouth,
To a place where he was known;
From there up to London,
To the place where he was born.

They took out his bowels,
And stretched out his feet,
And they balmed his body
With roses so sweet.

Six dukes stood before him,
Twelve raised him from the ground,
Nine lords followed after him
In their black mourning gown.

Black was their mourning,
And white were the wands,
And so yellow were the flamboys
That they carried in their hands.

He now lies betwixt two towers,
He now lies in cold clay,
And the Royal Queen of Grantham
Went weeping away.

The Cherry-Tree Carol

Joseph was an old man, and an old man was he,
When he wedded Mary, in the land of Galilee.

Joseph and Mary walked through an orchard good,
Where was cherries and berries, so red as any blood.

Joseph and Mary walked through an orchard green,
Where was berries and cherries, as thick as might be seen.

O then bespoke Mary, so meek and so mild:
'Pluck me one cherry, Joseph, for I am with child.'

O then bespoke Joseph, with words most unkind:
'Let him pluck thee a cherry that brought thee with child.'

O then bespoke the babe, within his mother's womb:
'Bow down then the tallest tree, for my mother to have some.'

151

Then bowed down the highest tree unto his mother's hand;
Then she cried, 'See, Joseph, I have cherries at command.'

O then bespake Joseph: 'I have done Mary wrong;
But cheer up, my dearest, and be not cast down.'

Then Mary plucked a cherry, as red as the blood,
Then Mary went home with her heavy load.

Then Mary took her babe, and sat him on her knee,
Saying, 'My dear son, tell me what this world will be.'

'O I shall be as dead, mother, as the stones in the wall;
O the stones in the streets, mother, shall mourn for me all.

'Upon Easter-day, mother, my uprising shall be;
O the sun and the moon, mother, shall both rise with me.'

The Bitter Withy

As it fell out on a Holy Day,
    The drops of rain did fall, did fall,
Our Saviour asked leave of His mother Mary
    If He might go play at ball.

'To play at ball, my own dear Son,
    It's time You was going or gone,
But be sure let me hear no complaint of You,
    At night when You do come home.'

It was upling scorn and downling scorn,
    Oh, there He met three jolly jerdins;
Oh, there He asked the jolly jerdins
    If they would go play at ball.

'Oh, we are lords' and ladies' sons,
  Born in bower or in hall,
And You are some poor maid's child
  Born'd in an ox's stall.'

'If you are lords' and ladies' sons,
  Born'd in bower or in hall,
Then at the last I'll make it appear
  That I am above you all.'

Our Saviour built a bridge with the beams of the sun,
  And over it He gone, He gone He.
And after followed the three jolly jerdins,
  And drownded they were all three.

It was upling scorn and downling scorn,
  The mothers of them did whoop and call,
Crying out, 'Mary mild, call home your Child,
  For ours are drownded all.'

Mary mild, Mary mild, called home her Child,
  And laid our Saviour across her knee,
And with a whole handful of bitter withy
  She gave him slashes three.

Then He says to His mother, 'Oh! the withy, oh! the withy,
  The bitter withy that causes me to smart, to smart,
Oh! the withy, it shall be the very first tree
  That perishes at the heart.'

Dives and Lazarus

As it fell out upon a day,
  Rich Dives he made a feast,
And he invited all his friends,
  And gentry of the best.

Then Lazarus laid him down and down,
    And down at Dives' door:
'Some meat, some drink, brother Dives,
    Bestow upon the poor.'

'Thou art none of my brother, Lazarus,
    That lies begging at my door;
No meat nor drink will I give thee,
    Nor bestow upon the poor.'

Then Lazarus laid him down and down,
    And down at Dives' wall:
'Some meat, some drink, brother Dives,
    Or with hunger starve I shall.'

'Thou art none of my brother, Lazarus,
    That lies begging at my wall;
No meat nor drink will I give thee,
    But with hunger starve you shall.'

Then Lazarus laid him down and down,
    And down at Dives' gate:
'Some meat, some drink, brother Dives,
    For Jesus Christ his sake.'

'Thou art none of my brother, Lazarus,
    That lies begging at my gate;
No meat nor drink will I give thee,
    For Jesus Christ his sake.'

Then Dives sent out his merry men,
    To whip poor Lazarus away;
They had no power to strike a stroke,
    But flung their whips away.

Then Dives sent out his hungry dogs,
   To bite him as he lay;
They had no power to bite at all,
   But licked his sores away.

As it fell out upon a day,
   Poor Lazarus sickened and died
Then came two angels out of heaven
   His soul therein to guide.

'Rise up, rise up, brother Lazarus,
   And go along with me;
For you've a place prepared in heaven,
   To sit on an angel's knee.'

As it fell out upon a day,
   Rich Dives sickened and died;
Then came two serpents out of hell,
   His soul therein to guide.

'Rise up, rise up, brother Dives,
   And go with us to see
A dismal place, prepared in hell,
   From which thou canst not flee.'

Then Dives looked up with his eyes,
   And saw poor Lazarus blest:
'Give me one drop of water, brother Lazarus,
   To quench my flaming thirst.

'Oh had I as many years to abide
   As there are blades of grass,
Then there would be an end, but now
   Hell's pains will ne'er be past.

'Oh was I now but alive again,
  The space of one half hour!
Oh that I had my peace secure!
  Then the devil should have no power.'

Sir John Barleycorn

There came three men from out of the west
Their victory to try;
And they have ta'en a solemn oath,
Poor Barleycorn should die.

They took a plough and ploughed him in,
Clods harrowed on his head;
And then they took a solemn oath
John Barleycorn was dead.

There he lay sleeping in the ground
Till rain on him did fall;
Then Barleycorn sprung up his head,
And so amazed them all.

There he remained till Midsummer
And look'd both pale and wan;
Then Barleycorn he got a beard
And so became a man.

Then they sent men with scythes so sharp
To cut him off at knee;
And then poor Johny Barleycorn
They served most barbarouslie.

Then they sent men with pitchforks strong
To pierce him through the heart;
And like a doleful Tragedy
They bound him in a cart.

And then they brought him to a barn
A prisoner to endure;
And so they fetched him out again,
And laid him on the floor.

Then they set men with holly clubs,
To beat the flesh from th' bones;
But the miller served him worse than that,
He ground him 'twixt two stones.

O! Barleycorn is the choicest grain
That e'er was sown on land:
It will do more than any grain
By the turning of your hand.

It will make a boy into a man,
A man into an ass:
To silver it will change your gold,
Your silver into brass.

It will make the huntsman hunt the fox,
That never wound a horn;
It will bring the tinker to the stocks
That people may him scorn.

O! Barleycorn is the choicest grain
That e'er was sown on land.
And it will cause a man to drink
Till he neither can go nor stand.

V

Broadside Ballads

A Ballade of the Scottyshe Kynge (1513)

JOHN SKELTON

Kyng Jamy/Jamy your Joye is all go
Ye sommnoed our kynge why dyde ye so?
To you nothyng it dyde accorde
To sommon our kynge your soverayne lorde.
A kynge a somner it is wonder
Knowe ye not salt and suger asonder?
In you sommynge ye were to malaperte
And your harolde no thynge experte.
Ye thought ye dyde it sull valyauntolye
But not worth thre skippes of a pye.
Syr quyer galyarde ye were to swyfte
Your wyll renne before your wytte.
To be so scornfull to your alye
Your counseyle was not worth a flye.
Before the frensshe kynge /danes/ and other
Ye ought to honour your lorde and brother.
Trowe ye syr James his noble grace
For you and your scottes wolde tourne his face
Now ye prode scottes of gelawaye
For your kynge may synge welawaye.
Now you must knowe our kynge for your regent
Your soverayne lorde and presedent
In hym is figured melchisedeche
And ye be desolate as armeleche.
He is our noble champyon
A kynge anoynted and ye be non,
Thrugh your counseyle your fader was slayne
Wherfore I fere ye wyll suffre payne
And ye proude scottes of dunbar
Parde ye be his homager

And suters to his parlyment
Ye dyde not your dewty therin.
Wyerfore ye may it now repent
Ye bere yourselfe som what to holde
Therfore ye have lost your copholde
Ye be bounde tenauntes to his estate
Gyve up your game ye playe chekmate
For to the castell of norham
I understonde to soone ye cam.
For a prysoner now ye be
Eyther to the devyll or the trinite.
Thanked be saynte Gorge our ladyes knythe
Your pryd is paste adwe good nyght.
Ye have determyned to make a fraye
Our kynge than beynge out of the waye
But by the power and myght of god
Ye were beten with your owne rod.
By your wanton wyll syr at a worde
Ye have lost spores, cote armure, and sworde
Ye had better to have busked to huntey bankes
Than in England to playe ony suche prankes
But ye had som wyle sede to sowe
Therefore ye be layde now full lowe,
Your power coude no longer atteyne
Warre with our kynge to meyntayne
Of the kyng of naverne ye may take hede
How unfortunately he doth now spede,
In double welles now he doeth dreme.
That is a kynge witou a realme
At hym example ye wolde none take
Experyence hath brought you in the same brake
Of the out yles ye rough foted scottes
We have well eased you of the bottes
Ye rowe ranke scottes and dronken danes
Of our englysshe bowes ye have fette your banes.

It is not syttynge in tour or towne
A somner to were a kynges crowne
That noble erle the whyte Lyon,
Your pompe and pryde hath layde a downe
His sone the lorde admyrall is full good
His swerd hath bathed in the scottes blode
God save kynge Henry and his lordes all
And sende the frensshe kynge suche an other fall
  Amen/for saynt charyte
  And god save noble
    Kynge/Henry/
      The VIII.

Whipping Cheare

(Or the wofull lamentations of the three Sisters
in the Spittle when they were in new Bride-well)

Come you fatall Sisters three,
whose exercise is spinning:
And helpe us to pull out these thrids,
for heer's but a harsh beginning.
  Oh hemp, and flax, and tow to to to,
  Tow to to to, tow tero.
  Oh hempe, etc.,

The blinded whipper hee attends us,
if the wheele leave turning,
And then the very Matrons lookes,
turnes all our mirth to mourning.
  Oh hempe and flax, and Tow to to to,
  tow to to to to to tero,
  Oh hempe etc.,

Now for a Cup of bottle Ale,
some suger-plummes and Cakes a,
But never a client must come in,
to giv's a poore pinte of Sacke.
  Heer's hemp and flax and tow to to to
  tow tow to to to to tero.
  Heer's hempe and etc.,

Besse the eldest Sister, shee
is slayned much with honour,
And one cannot endure the labour,
which is thrust upon her.
  O hemp and flax and tow to to to,
  Tow to to, to to tero.
  O hemp etc.,

Garden-allies cleare are swept,
Hog-laine laments a little:
Our tinder boxes over our heades,
were broken at the Spittle:
  Heer's hemp and flax and tow to to to,
  tow to to to to to tero.
  Heer's hempe etc.,

If the London Prentises,
And other good men of fashion:
Would but refraine our companies,
Then woe to our occupation.
  Then hempe and flaxe and tow to to to
  Tow to to to to tero.
  Then hempe etc.,

O you lusty Roring Boyes,
Come shew your brazen faces:
Let your weapons turn to beetles,
And shoulder out some of these lashes.

At hemp and flaxe and tow to to to,
Tow to to to to to tero.
At hemp etc.,

Gold and silver hath forsaken,
Our acquaintance cleerely:
Twined whipcord takes the place,
And strikes t'our shoulders neerely.
  Heer's hempe and flax and tow to to to,
  Tow to to to to tero.
  Heere's hemp etc.,

You Punkes and Panders everyone,
Come follow your loving sisters:
In new Bridewell there is a mill,
Fills all our hands with blisters.
  And hempe and flax and, tow to to to to tero.

If the Millers art you like not,
to the hempe blocke packe yee:
Thumpe, and thumpe, and thump apace,
for feare the whipper take yee.
  Ther's hemp, and flax and tow to to to,
  Tow to to to to tero.

The Journey into France

I came from *England* into *France*
Neither to learn to crindge, nor dance,
  Nor yett to ride, nor fence;
Nor for to doe such things as those
Who have return'd without a nose,
  They carried out from hence.

But I to Paris rode along,
Much like *John Dory* in the Song,
　　Upon a holy tide:
I on an ambling nagg did gett,
I hope itt is not paid for yett,
　　I spurr'd him on each side.

And to *St. Denis* first wee came
To see the sights at *Nostredame*,
　　The man that shews them snuffles:
Where who is apt for to beleive,
May see our Ladies right hand sleeve,
　　And her old Pantofles.

Her Haire, her Milke, her very Gowne,
Which shee did weare in *Bethleem* Towne,
　　When in the Inne shee lay:
Yet all the World know's that's a Fable,
For so good clothes ne're lay in Stable
　　Upon a lock of Hay.

No Carpenter could by his trade,
Gaine so much wealth as to have made
　　A Gowne of so riche stuffe:
Yet they (poore Fooles) thinke for Her creditt,
They must beleive old *Joseph* did itt,
　　'Cause Shee deserv'd enough.

There is the Lanthorne, which the *Jewes*
(When Judas ledd them foorth) did use,
　　Itt weighs my weight downe right:
But to beleive it you must thinke,
The *Jewes* did putt a candle in't,
　　And then 'twas wondrous light.

166

There is one of the Crosses Nailes,
Which who so sees his Bonnett vailes,
   And if hee list may kneele:
Some say it's false, 'twas never so,
Yet feeling itt thus much I know,
   Itt is as true as Steele.

There's one Saint there hath lost his Toes,
Another his Head, but not his Nose,
   A Finger and a Thumbe:
Now when wee had seene these holy raggs,
Wee went to th'Inne and tooke our naggs,
   And so away did come.

Wee came to *Paris* on the *Seane*,
It's wondrous Faire, but nothing Cleane,
   'Tis *Europes* Greatest Towne:
How strong itt is I need not tell itt,
For all the world may easily smell itt,
   That walke itt upp and downe.

There's many strange things for to see,
The Hospital, the Gallery,
   The Place Roiall doth excell:
The New Bridge and the Statues there,
At *Nostre-Dame St. Christopher*,
   The Steeple beares the Bell.

For Learning the University,
And for old Clothes the Frippery,
   The House the Queene did build:
St. Innocents, whose Earth devoures,
Dead corps in foure and twenty houres,
   And there the King was kill'd.

The *Bastile*, and *St. Dennis* sheete,
The *Shateele* much like *London* Fleete,
　The *Arsenall*, no toy:
But if you'le see the prettiest thing,
Go to the Court and see the King,
　Itt is a hopefull boy.

Hee is by all his Dukes and Peeres,
Reverencd as much for Witt as Yeares,
　Nor must you thinke itt much:
For Hee with little switch doth play,
And can make fine durt pies of clay,
　Oh never King made such.

A Bird that can but catch a fly,
Or prate, doth please his Majesty,
　'Tis knowne to every one:
The *Duke de Guise* gave him a Parrett,
And hee had twenty canons for itt,
　For his new Galeon.

Oh that I e're might have the happ,
To get the Bird which in the Mapp
　Wee call the *Indian Ruck*:
I'd give itt Him, and looke to bee
As Great and Wise as *Luinee*,
　Or else I had ill luck.

Birds round about his chamber stand,
And hee them feeds with his owne hand,
　'Tis his humility:
And if they doe lack anything,
They may but whistle for the King,
　And hee comes presently.

Now for these vertuous parts hee must
Entitled bee *Lewis the Just,*
 Great Henries rightfull Heire:
When to his Stile to adde more words,
You may better call Him King of Birds,
 Instead of lost *Navarre.*

He hath beside a pretty firke,
Taught him by Nature for to worke
 In yron with great ease:
Sometimes unto his forge hee goes,
And there hee puffs and there hee blows,
 And makes both Locks and Keies.

Which putts a doubt in every one,
Whether he were *Mars* or *Vulcans* sonne,
 Some few suspect his Mother:
Yet let them all say what they will,
I am resolv'd and will thinke still,
 As much the t'one as t'other.

His Queene's a pretty little Wench,
But borne in Spaine, speaks little French,
 Shee's ne're like to bee Mother:
For her incestuous house could not
Have any children but begott
 By Uncle or by Brother.

Now why should *Lewis* being so *Just*
Content himselfe to take his lust,
 On his Luina's mate:
And suffer his pretty little Queene,
From all her race that yett hath beene,
 So to degenerate.

'Twere Charity for to bee knowne,
To love others children as his owne,
    And keepe them: 'Tis no shame;
Unles that hee would greater bee,
Then was his Father King *Henry*,
    Who (men thought) did the same.

A Ballade upon a Wedding
SIR JOHN SUCKLING

I tell thee *Dick* where I have been,
Where I the rarest things have seen;
    Oh things without compare!
Such sights cannot be found
In any place on English ground
    Be it at Wake, or Fair.

At *Charing-Crosse*, hard by the way
Where we (thou know'st) do sell our Hay,
    There is a house with stairs;
And there did I see comming down
Such folks as are not in our Town,
    Vorty at least, in Pairs.

Amongst the rest, one Pest'lent fine,
(His beard no bigger though then thine)
    Walkt on before the rest:
Our Landlord looks like nothing to him:
The King (God blesse him) 'twould undo him
    Should he go still so drest.

At Course-a-Park, without all doubt,
He should have first been taken out
   By all the maids i'th Town:
Though lusty *Roger* there had been,
Or little *George* upon the Green,
    Or *Vincent* of the Crown.

But wot you what? the youth was going
To make an end of all his woing;
   The Parson for him staid:
Yet by his leave (for all his haste)
He did not so much wish all past
    (Perchance) as did the maid.

The maid (and thereby hangs a tale)
For such a maid no Whitson-ale
   Could ever yet produce:
No Grape that's kindly ripe, could be
So round, so plump, so soft as she,
    Nor half so full of Juyce.

Her finger was so small, the Ring
Would not stay on which they did bring,
   It was too wide a Peck:
And to say truth (for out it must)
It lookt like the great Collar (just)
    About our young Colt's neck.

Her feet beneath her Petticoat,
Like little mice stole in and out,
   As if they fear'd the light:
But oh! she dances such a way!
No sun upon an Easter day
   Is half so fine a sight.

171

He would have kist her once or twice,
But she would not, she was so nice,
   She would not do't in sight,
And then she lookt as who should say
I will do what I list today;
   And you shall do't at night.

Her Cheeks so rare a white was on,
No Dazy makes comparison,
   (Who sees them is undone)
For streaks of red were mingled there,
Such as on a Katherne Pear,
   (The side that's next the Sun.)

Her lips were red, and one was thin,
Compar'd to that was next her Chin;
   (Some Bee had stung it newly.)
But (*Dick*) her eyes so guard her face;
I durst no more upon them gaze
   Then on the sun in *July*.

Her mouth so small when she does speak,
Thou'dst swear her teeth her words did break
   That they might passage get,
But she so handled still the matter,
They came as good as ours, or better,
   And are not spent a whit.

If wishing should be any sin,
The Parson himself had guilty bin;
   (she lookt that day so purely,)
And did the Youth so oft the feat
At night, as some did in conceit,
   It would have spoiled him, surely.

Just in the nick the Cook knockt thrice,
And all the waiters in a trice
    His summons did obey,
Each serving man with dish in hand,
Marcht boldly up, like our Train Band,
    Presented, and away.

When all the meat was on the Table,
What man of knife, or teeth, was able
    To stay to be intreated?
And this the very reason was,
Before the Parson could say Grace
    The Company was seated.

The bus'nesse of the Kitchin's great,
For it is fit that men should eat;
    Nor was it there deni'd,
Passion oh me! how I run on!
There's that that would be thought upon,
    (I trow) besides the Bride.

Now hatts fly off, and youths carouse;
Healths first go round, and then the house,
    The Brides came thick and thick:
And when 'twas nam'd another health,
Perhaps he made it hers by stealth,
    (and who could help it? *Dick*)

O'th'sodain up they rise and dance;
Then sit again and sigh, and glance:
    Then dance again and kisse:
Thus sev'ral waies the time did passe,
Till ev'ry Woman wisht her place,
    And ev'ry Man wisht his.

By this time all were stoln aside
To counsel and undresse the Bride;
   But that he must not know:
But yet 'twas thought he ghest her mind
And did not mean to stay behind
   Above an hour or so.

When in he came (*Dick*) there she lay
Like new-faln snow melting away,
   ('Twas time I trow to part)
Kisses were now the onely stay,
Which soon she gave, as who would say,
   Good Boy! with all my heart.

But just as leav'ns would have to crosse it,
In came the Bridesmaids with the Posset:
   The Bridegroom eat in spight;
For had he left the Women to't
It would have cost two hours to do't,
   Which were too much that night.

At length the candles out and out,
All that they had not done, they do't;
   What that is, who can tell?
But I beleeve it was no more
Then thou and I have done before
   With *Bridget*, and with *Nell*.

A Proper New Ballad,
intituled The Fairies Farewell;
or, God-a-Mercy Will

RICHARD BISHOP CORBET

(To be sung or whistled, to the tune of *Meadow Brow* by the
learned; by the unlearned, to the tune of *Fortune*)

Farewell, rewards and Fairies,
  Good housewives now may say,
For now foul sluts in Dairies
  Do fare as well as they.
And though they sweep their hearths no less
  Than maids were wont to do,
Yet who of late for cleanliness,
  Finds Sixpence in her shoe?

Lament, lament, old Abbeys,
  The Fairies lost command;
They did but change Priest's babies,
  But some have chang'd your land:
And all your children stol'n from thence
  Are now grown puritans;
Who live as changelings ever since
  For love of your domains.

At morning and at evening both
  You merry were and glad,
So little care of sleep and sloth
  These pretty Ladies had;
When Tom came home from labour,
  Or Ciss to milking rose,
Then merrily merrily went their Tabor,
  And nimbly went their Toes.

Witness those rings and roundelayes
    Of theirs, which yet remain,
Were footed in Queen Mary's days
    On many a grassy plain;
But since of late, Elizabeth,
    And later James came in,
They never danced on any heath
    As when the time hath been.

By which we note the Fairies
    Were of the old profession;
Their songs were Ave Maries,
    Their dances were procession:
But now, alas! they all are dead
    Or gone beyond the Seas,
Or further for Religion fled,
    Or else they take their ease.

A tell-tale in their company
    They never could endure,
And whoso kept not secretly
    Their mirth was punished sure;
It was a just and Christian deed
    To pinch such black and blue:
O how the Common-wealth doth need
    Such Justices as you!

Now they have left their Quarters
    A Register they have,
Who looketh to their Charters
    A Man both wise and grave;
An hundred of their merry pranks
    By one that I could name
Are kept in store, con twenty thanks
    To William for the same.

To William Chourne of Staffordshire,
   Give laud and praises due;
Who every meal can mend your cheer,
   With tales both old and true;
To William all give audience,
   And pray you for his noddle;
For all the Fairies' evidence
   Were lost, if it were addle.

On the Lord Mayor and Court of Aldermen, presenting the late King and Duke of York each with a Copy of their Freedoms, Anno Dom. 1674

ANDREW MARVELL

The Londoners Gent to the King do present
   In a Box the City Maggot;
'Tis a thing full of weight, that requires the Might
   Of whole *Guild-Hall* Team to drag it.

Whilst their Church's unbuilt, and their Houses undwelt,
   And their Orphans want Bread to feed 'em;
Themselves they've bereft of the little Wealth they had left,
   To make an Offering of their Freedom.

O ye Addle brain'd Cits who henceforth in their Wits
   Would intrust their Youth to your heading;
When in Diamonds and Gold you have him thus enroll'd,
   You know both his Friends and his Breeding?

Beyond Sea he began, where such a Riot he ran,
   That every one there did leave him;
And now he's come O'er ten times worse than before,
   When none but such Fools would receive him.

He ne'er knew, not he, how to serve or be free,
    Though he has past through so many Adventures;
But e'er since he was bound, (that is he was crown'd)
    He has every Day broke his Indentures.

He spends all his Days in running to Plays,
    When he should in the Shop be poring:
And he wasts all his Nights in his constant Delights,
    Of Revelling, Drinking and Whoring.

Thro' out *Lumbard street* each Man he did meet,
    He would run on the *Score* and *borrow*,
When they'd ask'd for their own, he was broke and gone,
    And his Creditors left to Sorrow.

Though oft bound to the Peace, yet he never would cease,
    To vex his poor Neighbours with Quarrels,
And when he was beat, he still made his Retreat,
    To his *Cleavelands*, his *Nels*, and his *Carwels*.

Nay, his Company lewd, were twice grown so rude,
    That had not Fear taught him Sobriety,
And the House been well barr'd with Guard upon Guard,
    They had robb'd us of all our Propriety.

Such a Plot was laid, had not *Ashley* betray'd,
    As had cancell'd all Former Disasters;
And your Wives had been Strumpets to his Highnesses
        Trumpet,
    And Foot Boys had all been your Masters.

So many are the Debts, and the Bastards he gets,
    Which must all be defray'd by *London*,
That notwithstanding the Care of Sir *Thomas Player*,
    The Chamber must needs be undone.

His Words nor his Oath cannot bind him to Troth,
    And he values not Credit or History;
And though he has serv'd through two Prentships now,
    He knows not his Trade nor his Mystery.

Then *London* Rejoyce in thy fortunate Choice,
    To have made him free of thy Spices;
And do not mistrust he may once grow more just,
    When he's worn of his Follies and Vices.

And what little thing is that which you bring
    To the Duke, the Kingdom's Darling;
Ye hug it and draw like Ants at a Straw,
    Tho' too small for the Gristle of Starling.

Is it a Box of Pills to cure the Kings Ills?
    (He is too far gone to begin it)
Or that your fine Show in Processioning go,
    With the Pix and the Host within It.

The very first Head of the Oath you him read,
    Shews you all how fit he's to Govern,
When in Heart (you all knew) he ne'er was nor will be true,
    To his Country or to his Soveraign.

And who could swear, that he would forbear
    To cull out the good of an Alien,
Who still doth advance the Government of *France*,
    With a *Wife* and *Religion Italian*?

And now, Worshipful Sirs, go fold up your Furrs,
    And *Vyners* turn again, turn again!
I see who e'ers freed, you for Slaves are decreed
    Until you *burn again, burn again.*

The Dutchess of Monmouth's Lamentation
for the Loss of her Duke

'Loyal Hearts of *London* City, Come I pray, and sing my
      Ditty,
    Of my Love that's from me gone;
I am slighted and much spighted, and am left alone to mourn.

'Was not that a dreadful thing, To make a Plot against the
      King,
    And his Royal Brother too?
I am vexed and perplexed, for my dear that prov'd untrue.

'A Hellish Plot there was contrived, and then at last they were
      devised
    To make it known unto the King,
How they had plotted and alloted a Murther then for to kill
      him.

'But *Shaftsbury* and his wits confounded, that had my *Jemmy*
      so be rounded
    For to Conspire against his King,
But God Direct and him Protect, that they may never Murther
      him.

'My Jemmy was a Subject Royal, But now has prov'd himself
      Disloyal';
    (Then she cryed out a main)
'My heart will break, for my Love's sake, Because he ne're will
      come again.

'*Jemmy* now is prov'd a Traytor, *Tony* and he were so sad
Creatures,
For to meddle so with things,
That were too high: proud *Shaftsbury*, For him to meddle so
with Kings!

'*Shaftsbury* was wondrous witty, to ruin three Nations, more's
the pitty!
Of it he was very shy;
But he is fled, and is since dead, that did disturb true *Monarchy*.

'*Jemmy* once was Loyal-hearted, And would his Life soon
apparted
For his King and Nation's good;
He delighting all in fighting, Made his peace where 'ere he stood.

'*Shaftsbury*, he was a Rebbel, Unto the King he was uncivil,
For all the Honour he did gain;
The King he slighted, and much spighted, And so he did his
Royal Train.

'*Jemmy* was a Foe to no Man, Till wheedl'd in by *Shaftsbury*,
Till at last he was forc'd to fly:
You know the Reason, 'twas for Treason, For disturbing
Monarchy.

'The Horrid Plot that they were known, Then against the King
and Crown,
That makes my Heart to Bleed full sad,
For to hear my only dear were lately grown so very bad.

'All my joys are gone and blasted. I with grief am almost
wasted,
For my *Jemmy* that's to me dear.'
Then from her Eyes, with fresh supplies, down trickles many a
brackish Tear.

'God bless the King and his Royal Brother, And keep us from
     such horrid murther,
  That were contriv'd by *Shaftsbury*
He was a Wretch fit for *Jack Ketch*; for disturbing of *Monarchy*!'

Now she ends her doleful story, Her Lamentation's laid before
     ye,
  She laments for her own Dear,
Then from her Eyes, with fresh supplies, down trickles many a
     brinish Tear.

Clever Tom Clinch going to be Hanged (1726)

JONATHAN SWIFT

As clever *Tom Clinch*, while the Rabble was bawling,
Rode stately through *Holbourn*, to die in his Calling;
He stopt at the *George* for a Bottle of Sack,
And promis'd to pay for it when he'd come back.
His Waistcoat and Stockings, and Breeches were white,
His Cap had a new Cherry Ribbon to ty't.
The Maids to the Doors and the Balconies ran,
And said, lack-a-day! he's a proper young Man.
But, as from the Windows the Ladies he spy'd,
Like a Beau in the Box, he bow'd low on each Side;
And when his last Speech the loud Hawkers did cry,
He swore from his Cart, it was all a damn'd Lye.
The Hangman for Pardon fell down on his Knee;
Tom gave him a Kick in the Guts for his Fee.
Then said, I must speak to the People a little,
But I'll see you all damn'd before I will *whittle*.
My honest Friend *Wild*, may he long hold his Place,
He lengthen'd my Life with a whole Year of Grace.
Take Courage, dear Comrades, and be not afraid,
Nor slip this Occasion to follow your Trade.

My Conscience is clear, and my Spirits are calm,
And thus I go off without Pray'r-Book or Psalm.
Then follow the Patience of clever *Tom Clinch*,
Who hung like a Hero, and never would flinch.

Newgate's Garland

being

A New Ballad,

showing how Mr. Jonathan Wild's throat was cut from ear to
ear with a penknife, by Mr. Blake, *alias* Blueskin, the bold
highwayman, as he stood at his trial in the Old Bailey, 1725
To the tune of *The Cut-Purse*

Ye gallants of Newgate, whose fingers are nice,
In diving in pockets, or cogging of dice,
Ye sharpers so rich, who can buy off the noose,
Ye honester poor rogues, who die in your shoes,
   Attend and draw near,
   Good news you shall hear,
   How Jonathan's throat was cut from ear to ear;
How Blueskin's sharp penknife hath set you at ease,
And every man round me may rob if he please.

When to the Old Bailey this Blueskin was led,
He held up his hand, the indictment was read,
Loud rattled his chains, near him Jonathan stood,
For full forty pounds was the price of his blood.
   Then hopeless of life,
   He drew his penknife,
   And made a sad widow of Jonathan's wife.
But forty pounds paid her, her grief shall appease,
And every man round me may rob if he please.

183

Knaves of old, to hide guilt by their cunning inventions,
Call'd briberies grants, and plain robberies pensions;
Physicians and lawyers (who take their degrees
To be learned rogues) call'd their pilfering fees;
 Since this happy day,
 Now every man may
 Rob (as safe in office) upon the highway.
For Blueskin's sharp penknife hath set you at ease,
And every man round me may rob if he please.

Some cheat in the customs, some rob the excise,
But he who robs both is esteemed most wise.
Church-wardens, too prudent to hazard the halter,
As yet only venture to steal from the altar:
 But now to get gold,
 They may be more bold,
 And rob on the highway, since Jonathan's cold.
For Blueskin's sharp penknife hath set you at ease,
And every man round me may rob if he please.

Some by public revenues which pass'd through their hands,
Have purchased clean houses and bought dirty lands;
Some to steal from a charity think it no sin,
Which at home (says the proverb) does always begin.
 But if ever you be
 Assign'd a trustee
 Treat not orphans like Masters of the Chancery.
But take the highway and more honestly seize,
For every man round me may rob if he please.

What a pother has here been with Wood and his brass
Who would modestly make a few halfpennies pass.
The patient is good, and the precedent's old.
For Diomede changèd his copper for gold.

But if Ireland despise
  Thy new halfpennies,
  With more safety to rob on the road I advise;
For Blueskin's sharp penknife hath set thee at ease,
And every man round me may rob if he please.

The Fine Old English Gentleman (1841)

CHARLES DICKENS

New Version

To be said or sung at all Conservative Dinners

I'll sing you a new ballad, and I'll warrant it first-rate,
Of the days of that old gentleman who had that old estate;
When they spent the public money at a bountiful old rate
On ev'ry mistress, pimp, and scamp, at ev'ry noble gate,
    In the fine old English Tory times;
    Soon may they come again!

The good old laws were garnished well with gibbets, whips, and
        chains,
With fine old English penalties, and fine old English pains,
With rebel heads, and seas of blood once hot in rebel veins;
For all these things were requisite to guard the rich old gains
    Of the fine old English Tory times;
    Soon may they come again!

This brave old code, like Argus, had a hundred watchful eyes,
And ev'ry English peasant had his good old English spies,
To tempt his starving discontent with fine old English lies,
Then call the good old Yeomanry to stop his peevish cries,
    In the fine old English Tory times;
    Soon may they come again!

The good old times for cutting throats that cried out in their
        need,
The good old times for hunting men who held their fathers'
        creed,
The good old times when William Pitt, as all good men agreed,
Came down direct from Paradise at more than railroad
        speed. . . .
    Oh the fine old English Tory times;
    When will they come again!

In those rare days, the press was seldom known to snarl or bark,
But sweetly sang of men in pow'r, like any tuneful lark;
Grave judges, too, to all their evil deeds were in the dark;
And not a man in twenty score knew how to make his mark.
    Oh the fine old English Tory times;
    Soon may they come again!

Those were the days for taxes, and for war's infernal din;
For scarcity of bread, that fine old dowagers might win;
For shutting men of letters up, through iron bars to grin,
Because they didn't think the Prince was altogether thin,
    In the fine old English Tory times;
    Soon may they come again!

But Tolerance, though slow in flight, is strong-wing'd in the
        main;
That night must come on these fine days, in course of time was
        plain;
The pure old spirit struggled, but its struggles were in vain;
A nation's grip was on it, and it died in choking pain,
    With the fine old English Tory days,
    All of the olden time.

The bright old day now dawns again; the cry runs through the
    land,
In England there shall be dear bread—in Ireland, sword and
    brand;
And poverty, and ignorance, shall swell the rich and grand,
So, rally round the rulers with the gentle iron hand,
    Of the fine old English Tory days;
    Hail to the coming time!

A New Song on the Birth of the Prince of Wales

Who was born on Tuesday, November 9, 1841

There's a pretty fuss and bother both in country and in town,
Since we have got a present, and an heir unto the Crown,
A little Prince of Wales so charming and so sly,
And the ladies shout with wonder, What a pretty little boy!

He must have a little musket, a trumpet and a kite,
A little penny rattle, and silver sword so bright,
A little cap and feather with scarlet coat so smart,
And a pretty little hobby horse to ride about the park.

Prince Albert he will often take the young Prince on his lap,
And fondle him so lovingly while he stirs about the pap,
He will pin on his flannel before he takes his nap,
Then dress him out so stylish with his little clouts and cap.

He must have a dandy suit to strut about the town,
John Bull must rake together six or seven thousand pound,
You'd laugh to see his daddy, at night he homewards runs,
With some peppermint or lollipops, sweet cakes and sugar
  plums.

He will want a little fiddle, and a little German flute,
A little pair of stockings and a pretty pair of boots,
With a handsome pair of spurs, and a golden headed cane,
And a stick of barley sugar, as long as Drury Lane.

An old maid ran through the palace, which did the nobs
    surprize,
Bawling out, he's got his daddy's mouth, his mammy's nose and
    eyes,
He will be as like his daddy as a frigate to a ship,
If he'd only got mustachios upon his upper lip.

Now to get these little niceties the taxes must be rose,
For the little Prince of Wales wants so many suits of clothes,
So they must tax the frying pan, the windows and the doors,
The bedsteads and the tables, kitchen pokers, and the floors.

Life of the Mannings

(Executed at Horsemonger Lane Gaol on Tuesday,
13 November, 1849)

See the scaffold it is mounted,
  And the doomed ones do appear,
Seemingly borne wan with sorrow,
  Grief and anguish, pain and care.
They cried, the moment is approaching,
  When we, together, must leave this life,
And no one has the least compassion
  On Frederick Manning and his wife.

Maria Manning came from Sweden,
  Brought up respectably, we hear,
And Frederick Manning came from Taunton,
  In the county of Somersetshire.

Maria lived with noble ladies,
In ease and splendour and delight,
But on one sad and fatal morning,
She was made Frederick Manning's wife.

She first was courted by O'Connor,
Who was a lover most sincere,
He was possessed of wealth and riches,
And loved Maria Roux most dear.
But she preferred her present husband,
As it appeared, and with delight,
Slighted sore Patrick O'Connor,
And was made Frederick Manning's wife.

And when O'Connor knew the story,
Down his cheeks rolled floods of tears,
He beat his breast and wept in sorrow,
Wrung his hands and tore his hair;
Maria, dear, how could you leave me?
Wretched you have made my life,
Tell me why you did deceive me,
For to be Fred Manning's wife?

At length they were all reconciled,
And met together night and day,
Maria, by O'Connor's riches,
Dressed in splendour fine and gay.
Though married, yet she corresponded
With O'Connor, all was right,
And oft he went to see Maria,
Frederick Manning's lawful wife.

At length they plann'd their friend to murder,
And for his company did crave,
The dreadful weapons they prepared,
And in the kitchen dug his grave.

And, as they fondly did caress him,
They slew him—what a dreadful sight,
First they mangled, after robbed him,
Frederick Manning and his wife.

They absconded but were apprehended,
And for the cruel deed were tried,
When placed at the Bar of Newgate,
They both the crime strongly denied.
At length the Jury them convicted,
And doomed them for to leave this life,
The Judge pronounced the awful sentence,
On Frederick Manning, and his wife.

Return, he said, to whence they brought you,
From thence unto the fatal tree,
And there together be suspended,
Where multitudes your fate may see.
Your hours, recollect, are numbered,
You betrayed a friend, and took his life,
For such there's not one spark of pity,
For Frederick Manning and his wife.

See what numbers are approaching,
To Horse Monger's fatal tree,
Full of blooming health and vigour,
What a dreadful sight to see.
Old and young, pray take a warning,
Females, lead a virtuous life,
Think upon that fatal morning,
Frederick Manning and his wife.

Wednesbury Cocking

At Wednesbury there was a cocking,
    A match between Newton and Scroggins;
The colliers and nailers left work,
    And all to old Spittle's went jogging.
To see this noble sport,
    Many noblemen resorted;
And though they'd but little money,
    Yet that little they freely sported.

There was Jeffret and Colborn from Hampton,
    And Dusty from Bilston was there;
Plummery he came from Darlaston,
    And he was as rude as a bear.
There was old Will from Walsall,
    And Smacker from Westbromwich come;
Blind Robin he came from Rowley,
    And staggering he went home.

Ralph Moody came hobbling along,
    As though he some cripple were mocking,
To join in the blackguard throng,
    That met at Wednesbury cocking.
He borrowed a rifle of Doll,
    To back old Taverner's grey;
He laid fourpence-halfpenny to fourpence,
    He lost and went broken away.

But soon he returned to the pit,
    For he'd borrowed a trifle more money,
And ventured another large bet,
    Along with blubbermouth Coney.

191

When Coney demanded his money,
    As is common on all such occasions,
He cried: 'Rot thee, if thee don't hold thy rattle,
    I'll pay thee as Paul paid the Ephesians.'

Scroggins' breeches were made of nankeen,
    And worn very thin in the groin,
When he stooped to handle a cock,
    His buttocks burst out behind!
Besides, his shirt tail was all beshet,
    Which caused among them much laughter,
Scroggins turned around in a pet,
    And cried: 'Damn ye all, what's the matter?'

The morning's sport being over,
    Old Spittle a dinner proclaimed,
Each man he should dine for a groat,
    If he grumbled he ought to be maimed.
For there was plenty of beef,
    But Spittle he swore by his troth
That never a man should dine
    Till he'd ate his noggin of broth.

The beef it was old and tough,
    Of a bull that was baited to death,
Barney Hyde got a lump in his throat,
    That had like to have stopped his breath;
The company all fell in confusion,
    At seeing poor Barney Hyde choke,
So they took him into the kitchen,
    And held him over the smoke.

They held him so close to the fire,
    He frizzled just like a beefsteak,
They then threw him down on the floor,
    Which had like to have broken his neck.

One gave him a kick in the stomach,
    Another a clout on the brow,
His wife said: 'Throw him into the stable,
    And he'll be better just now.'

Then they all returned to the pit,
    And the fighting went forward again;
Six battles were fought on each side,
    And the next was to decide the main.
For these were two famous cocks
    As ever this country bred,
Scroggins a duck-winged black,
    And Newton's a shift-winged red.

The conflict was hard on both sides,
    Till Brassy's shift-winged was choked;
The colliers were tarnationly vexed,
    And the nailers were sorely provoked.
Peter Stevens he swore a great oath
    That Scroggins had played his cock foul;
Scroggins gave him a kick on the head,
    And cried: 'Yea, God damn thy soul!'

The company then fell in discord,
    A bold, bold fight did ensue;
Kick, bludgeon and bite was the word,
    Till the Walsall men were all subdued.
Ralph Moody bit off a man's nose,
    And wished that he could have him slain,
So they trampled both cocks to death,
    And they made a draw of the main.

The cock-pit was near to the church,
    An ornament unto the town;
On one side an old coal pit,
    The other well gorsed around.

Peter Hadley peeped through the gorse,
    In order to see the cocks fight;
Spittle jobbed out his eye with a fork,
    And said: 'Rot thee, it served thee right!'

Some people may think this strange,
    Who Wednesbury Town never knew;
But those who have ever been there,
    Won't have the least doubt it is true;
For they are so savage by nature,
    And guilty of deeds the most shocking;
Jack Baker he whacked his own father,
    And thus ended Wednesbury Cocking.

Miss Bailey's Ghost

A captain bold, in Halifax, who dwelt in country quarters,
Seduced a maid, who hang'd herself, one morning, in her garters,
His wicked conscience smited him, he lost his stomach daily,
He took to drinking ratafee, and thought upon Miss Bailey.
Oh, Miss Bailey! unfortunate Miss Bailey.

One night betimes he went to rest, for he had caught a fever,
Says he, 'I am a handsome man, but I'm a gay deceiver;'
His candle just at twelve o'clock began to burn quite palely,
A ghost stepp'd up to his bedside, and said, 'behold Miss
    Bailey.'
Oh, Miss Bailey! unfortunate Miss Bailey.

'Avaunt, Miss Bailey,' then he cried, 'your face looks white and
    mealy,'
'Dear Captain Smith,' the ghost replied, 'you've used me
    ungenteely;

The Crowner's Quest goes hard with me, because I've acted
    frailly,
And parson Biggs won't bury me, though I am dead Miss
    Bailey.'
Oh, Miss Bailey! unfortunate Miss Bailey.

'Dear Corpse,' said he, 'since you and I accounts must once for
    all close,
I've really got a one pound note in my regimental small clothes;
'Twill bribe the sexton for your grave.'—The ghost then
    vanish'd gaily,
Crying 'Bless you, wicked Captain Smith, remember poor Miss
    Bailey.'
Oh, Miss Bailey! unfortunate Miss Bailey.

Danny Deever
RUDYARD KIPLING

'What are the bugles blowin' for ?' said Files-on-Parade.
'To turn you out, to turn you out,' the Colour-Sergeant said.
'What makes you look so white, so white ?' said Files-on-Parade.
'I'm dreadin' what I've got to watch,' the Colour-Sergeant said.
  For they're hangin' Danny Deever, you can hear the Dead
    March play,
  The regiment's in 'ollow square—they're hangin' him today;
  They've taken of his buttons off an' cut his stripes away,
  An' they're hangin' Danny Deever in the mornin'.

'What makes the rear-rank breathe so 'ard ?' said Files-on
    Parade.
'It's bitter cold, it's bitter cold,' the Colour-Sergeant said.
'What makes that front-rank man fall down ?' says Files-on-
    Parade.
'A touch o' sun, a touch o' sun,' the Colour-Sergeant said.

They are hangin' Danny Deever, they are marchin' of 'im
    round,
They 'ave 'alted Danny Deever by 'is coffin on the ground;
An' 'e'll swing in 'arf a minute for a sneakin' shootin' hound—
O they're hangin' Danny Deever in the mornin'.

"Is cot was right-'and cot to mine,' said Files-on-Parade.
"E's sleepin' out and far to-night,' the Colour-Sergeant said.
'I've drunk 'is beer a score o' times,' said Files-on-Parade.
"E's drinkin' bitter beer alone,' the Colour-Sergeant said.
    They are hangin' Danny Deever, you must mark 'im to 'is
        place
    For 'e shot a comrade sleepin'—you must look 'im in the face;
    Nine 'undred of 'is county an' the regiment's disgrace,
    While they're hangin' Danny Deever in the mornin'.

'What's that so black agin the sun?' said Files-on-Parade.
'It's Danny fightin' 'ard for life,' the Colour-Sergeant said.
'What's that that whimpers over'ead?' said Files-on-Parade.
'It's Danny's soul that's passin' now,' the Colour-Sergeant said.
    For they're done with Danny Deever, you can 'ear the
        quickstep play,
    The regiment's in column, an' they're marchin' us away;
    Ho! the young recruits are shakin' an' they'll want their beer
        to-day
    After hangin' Danny Deever in the mornin'.

VI

Irish

Brian O Linn

Brian O Linn had no breeches to wear,
He got an old sheepskin to make him a pair,
With the fleshy side out and the woolly side in,
'They'll be pleasant and cool,' says Brian O Linn.

Brian O Linn had no shirt to his back,
He went to a neighbour's, and borrowed a sack,
Then he puckered the meal bag in under his chin,
'Sure they'll take them for ruffles,' says Brian O Linn.

Brian O Linn was hard up for a coat,
So he borrowed the skin of a neighbouring goat,
With the horns sticking out from his oxsters, and then,
'Sure they'll take them for pistols,' says Brian O Linn.

Brian O Linn had no hat to put on,
So he got an old beaver to make him a one,
There was none of the crown left and less of the brim,
'Sure there's fine ventilation,' says Brian O Linn.

Brian O Linn had no brogues for his toes,
He hopped in two crab-shells to serve him for those.
Then he split up two oysters that match'd like a twin,
'Sure they'll shine out like buckles,' says Brian O Linn.

Brian O Linn had no watch to put on,
So he scooped out a turnip to make him a one.
Then he placed a young cricket in-under the skin,
'Sure they'll think it is ticking,' says Brian O Linn.

Brian O Linn to his house had no door,
He'd the sky for a roof, and the bog for a floor;
He'd a way to jump out, and a way to swim in,
''Tis a fine habitation,' says Brian O Linn.

Brian O Linn went a-courting one night,
He set both the mother and daugher to fight;
To fight for his hand they both stripped to the skin,
'Sure! I'll marry you both,' says Brian O Linn.

Brian O Linn, his wife and wife's mother,
They all lay down in the bed together,
The sheets they were old and the blankets were thin,
'Lie close to the wall,' says Brian O Linn.

Brian O Linn, his wife and wife's mother,
Were all going home o'er the bridge together,
The bridge it broke down, and they all tumbled in,
'We'll go home by the water,' says Brian O Linn.

The Bonny Bunch of Roses

By the margin of the ocean, one pleasant evening in the month
of June,
When all those feathered songsters their liquid notes did
sweetly tune,
'Twas there I spied a female, and on her features signs of woe,
Conversing with young Bonaparte, concerning the Bonny
Bunch of Roses, O.

Then up speaks young Napoleon, and takes his mother by the
hand,
Saying: 'Mother dear, be patient until I'm able to take
command;
And I'll raise a mighty army, and through tremendous dangers
go,
And I never will return again till I've conquered the Bonny
Bunch of Roses, O.

IRISH

'When first you saw great Bonaparte, you fell upon your
bended knee,
And you asked your father's life of him, he granted it right
manfully.
And 'twas then he took his army, and o'er the frozen Alps did
go,
And he said: 'I'll conquer Moscow, and return for the Bonny
Bunch of Roses, O.'

'He took three hundred thousand men, and kings likewise to
bear his train,
He was so well provided for, that he could sweep the world for
gain;
But when he came to Moscow, he was overpowered by the sleet
and snow,
With Moscow all a-blazing, and he lost the Bonny Bunch of
Roses, O.'

'Now son, be not too venturesome, for England is the heart of
oak,
And England, Ireland, Scotland, their unity shall ne'er be
broke;
Remember your brave father, in Saint Helena he lies low,
And if you follow after, beware of the Bonny Bunch of Roses,
O.'

'O mother, adieu for ever, for now I lie on my dying bed,
If I lived I'd have been clever, but now I droop my youthful
head;
But when our bones lie mouldering and weeping willows o'er us
grow,
The name of young Napoleon will enshrine the Bonny Bunch of
Roses, O.'

Dunlavin Green

In the year of one thousand seven hundred and ninety eight,
A sorrowful tale the truth unto you I'll relate.
Of thirty-six heroes to the world were left to be seen,
By a false information were shot on Dunlavin Green.

Bad luck to you, Saunders, for you did their lives betray;
You said a parade would be held on that very day,
Our drums they did rattle—our fifes they did sweetly play;
Surrounded we were and privately marched away.

Quite easy they led us as prisoners through the town,
To be slaughtered on the plain, we then were forced to kneel
        down,
Such grief and such sorrow were never before there seen,
When the blood ran in streams down the dykes of Dunlavin
        Green.

There is young Matty Farrell, has plenty of cause to complain,
Also the two Duffys, who were shot down on the plain,
And young Andy Ryan, his mother distracted will run
For her own brave boy, her beloved eldest son.

Bad luck to you, Saunders, bad luck may you never shun!
That the widow's curse may melt you like snow in the sun,
The cries of the orphans whose murmurs you cannot screen,
For the murder of their dear fathers, on Dunlavin Green.

Some of our boys to the hills they are going away,
Some of them are shot, and some of them going to sea,
Micky Dwyer in the mountains to Saunders he owes a spleen,
For his loyal brothers, who were shot on Dunlavin Green.

The Croppy Boy

It was early, early in the spring,
The birds did whistle and sweetly sing,
Changing their notes from tree to tree,
And the song they sang was Old Ireland free.

It was early, early in the night,
The yeoman cavalry gave me a fright;
The yeoman cavalry was my downfall
And taken was I by Lord Cornwall.

'Twas in the guard-house where I was laid
And in a parlour where I was tried;
My sentence passed and my courage low
When to Dungannon I was forced to go.

As I was passing my father's door
My brother William stood at the door,
My aged father stood at the door
And my tender mother her hair she tore.

As I was walking up Wexford Street
My own first cousin I chanced to meet;
My own first cousin did me betray,
And for one bare guinea swore my life away.

My sister Mary heard the express,
She ran upstairs in her morning-dress—
Five hundred guineas I will lay me down,
To see my brother safe in Wexford town.

As I was walking up Wexford Hill,
Who could blame me to cry my fill?

I looked behind me and I looked before,
But my tender mother I shall ne'er see more.

As I was mounted on the platform high,
My aged father was standing by;
My aged father did me deny,
And the name he gave me was the Croppy Boy.

It was in Dungannon this young man died,
And in Dungannon his body lies;
And you good Christians that do pass by,
Just shed a tear for the Croppy Boy.

Brennan on the Moor

It's of a fearless highwayman a story now I'll tell:
His name was Willie Brennan, and in Ireland he did dwell;
'Twas on the Limerick mountains he commenced his wild career,
Where many a wealthy gentleman before him shook with fear;
    Brennan on the moor, Brennan on the moor,
    Bold and yet undaunted stood young Brennan on the moor.

A brace of loaded pistols he carried night and day,
He never robb'd a poor man upon the King's highway;
But what he's taken from the rich, like Turpin and Queen Bess,
He always did divide it with the widow in distress.

One night he robbed a packman, his name was Pedlar Bawn;
They travelled on together, till day began to dawn;
The pedlar seeing his money gone, likewise his watch and chain,
He at once encountered Brennan and robbed him back again.

When Brennan saw the pedlar was as good a man as he,
He took him on the highway, his companion for to be;
The pedlar threw away his pack without any more delay,
And proved a faithful comrade until his dying day.

One day upon the highway Willie he sat down,
He met the Mayor of Cashel, a mile outside the town;
The Mayor he knew his features, 'I think, young man,' said he,
'Your name is Willie Brennan, you must come along with me.'

As Brennan's wife had gone to town provisions for to buy,
When she saw her Willie, she began to weep and cry;
He says, 'Give me that tenpence;' as soon as Willie spoke,
She handed him the blunderbuss from underneath her cloak.

Then with his loaded blunderbuss, the truth I will unfold,
He made the Mayor to tremble, and robbed him of his gold;
One hundred pounds was offered for his apprehension there,
And with his horse and saddle to the mountains did repair.

Then Brennan being an outlaw upon the mountain high,
Where cavalry and infantry to take him they did try,
He laughed at them with scorn, until at length, it's said,
By a false-hearted young man he was basely betrayed.

In the County of Tipperary, in a place they called Clonmore,
Willie Brennan and his comrade that day did suffer sore;
He lay among the fern which was thick upon the field,
And nine wounds he had received before that he did yield.

Then Brennan and his companion knowing they were betrayed,
He with the mounted cavalry a noble battle made;
He lost his foremost finger, which was shot off by a ball;
So Brennan and his comrades they were taken after all.

So they were taken prisoners, in irons they were bound,
And conveyed to Clonmel jail, strong walls did them surround;
They were tried and found guilty, the judge made this reply.
'For robbing on the King's highway you are both condemned to
    die.'

Farewell unto my wife, and to my children three,
Likewise my aged father, he may shed tears for me.
And to my loving mother, who tore her gray locks and cried,
Saying 'I wish, Willie Brennan, in your cradle you had died.'

Young Molly Bán

Come all you young fellows that follow the gun,
Beware of goin' a-shootin' by the late setting sun.
It might happen to anyone as it happened to me,
To shoot your own true love in-under a tree.

She was going to her uncle's, when the shower it came on,
She went under a bush, the rain for to shun.
With her apron all around her, I took her for a swan
And I levelled my gun and I shot Molly Bán.

I ran to her uncle's in haste and great fear,
Saying Uncle, dear Uncle, I've shot Molly dear.
With her apron all around her I took her for a swan,
But oh and alas! it was my Molly Bán.

I shot my own true love—alas I'm undone,
While she was in the shade by the setting of the sun;
If I thought she was there I'd caress her tenderly,
And soon I'd get married to my own dear Molly.

My curses on you, Toby, that lent me your gun
To go out a-shooting by the late setting sun,
I rubbed her fair temples and found she was dead;
A fountain of tears for my Molly I shed.

Up comes my father and his locks they were grey,
Stay in your own country and don't run away,
Stay in your own country till your trial comes on,
And I'll see you set free by the laws of the land.

Oh the maids of this country they will all be very glad
When they hear the sad news that my Molly is dead.
Take them all in their hundreds, set them all in a row,
Molly Bán she shone above them like a mountain of snow.

The Rocky Road to Dublin

In the merry month of May from my home I started,
Left the girls of Tuam nearly broken hearted,
Saluted father dear, kissed my darlin' mother,
Drank a pint of beer, my grief and tears to smother,
Then off to reap the corn, and leave where I was born,
I cut a stout blackthorn, to banish ghost and goblin,
In a bran new pair of brogues, I rattled o'er the bogs,
And frightened all the dogs on the Rocky road to Dublin.
> *One, two, three, four, five,*
> *Hunt the hare and turn her*
> *Down the rocky road and all the ways to Dublin,*
> *Whack-fol-lol-de-ra.*

In Mullingar that night I rested limbs so weary,
Started by daylight next mornin' light and airy,
Took a drop of the pure, to keep my heart from sinkin',
That's an Irishman's cure, whene'er he's on for drinking.
To see the lasses smile, laughing all the while,
At my curious style, 'twould set your heart a-bubblin'.
They ax'd if I was hired, the wages I required,
Till I was almost tired of the rocky road to Dublin.

In Dublin next arrived, I thought it such a pity,
To be so soon deprived a view of that fine city.
Then I took a stroll all among the quality,
My bundle it was stole in a neat locality;
Something crossed my mind, then I looked behind
No bundle could I find upon my stick a wobblin'.

Enquirin' for the rogue, they said my Connacht brogue,
Wasn't much in vogue on the rocky road to Dublin.

From there I got away, my spirits never failin'
Landed on the quay as the ship was sailin';
Captain at me roared, said that no room had he,
When I jumped aboard, a cabin found for Paddy.
Down among the pigs I played some funny rigs,
Danced some hearty jigs, the water round me bubblin'.
When off Holyhead, I wished myself was dead,
Or better far instead, on the rocky road to Dublin.

The boys of Liverpool, when we safely landed,
Called myself a fool, I could no longer stand it;
Blood began to boil, temper I was losin',
Poor ould Erin's isle they began abusin',
'Hurrah my soul', sez I, my shillelagh I let fly;
Some Galway boys were by, saw I was a hobble in,
Then with a loud hurrah, they joined in the affray.
We quickly cleared the way, for the rocky road to Dublin.
> *One, two, three, four, five,*
> *Hunt the hare and turn her*
> *Down the rocky road and all the way to Dublin.*
> *Whack-fol-lol-de-ra.*

The Night before Larry was Stretched

The night before Larry was stretched,
The boys they all paid him a visit;
A bit in their sacks, too, they fetched;
They sweated their duds till they riz it;
For Larry was ever the lad,
When a boy was condemned to the squeezer,
Would fence all the duds that he had
To help a poor friend to a sneezer,
And warm his gob 'fore he died.

The boys they came crowding in fast,
They drew all their stools round about him,
Six glims round his trap-case were placed,
He couldn't be well waked without 'em.
When one of us asked could he die
Without having truly repented,
Says Larry, 'That's all in my eye,
And first by the clergy invented,
To get a fat bit for themselves.'

'I'm sorry, dear Larry,' says I,
'To see you in this situation;
And, blister my limbs if I lie,
I'd as lieve it had been my own station.'
'Ochone! it's all over,' says he,
'For the neck-cloth I'll be forced to put on,
And by this time tomorrow you'll see
Your poor Larry as dead as a mutton,
Because why, his courage was good.

'And I'll be cut up like a pie,
And my nob from my body be parted.'
'You're in the wrong box, then,' says I,
'For blast me if they're so hard-hearted;
A chalk on the back of your neck
Is all that Jack Ketch dares to give you;
Then mind not such trifles a feck,
For why should the likes of them grieve you?
And now, boys, come tip us the deck.'

The cards being called for, they played,
Till Larry found one of them cheated;
A dart at his napper he made
(The boy being easily heated);

o

IRISH

'O, by the hokey, you thief,
I'll scuttle your nob with my daddle!
You cheat me because I'm in grief,
But soon I'll demolish your noddle,
And leave you your claret to drink.'

Then the clargy came in with his book,
He spoke him so smooth and so civil;
Larry pitched him a Kilmainham look,
And pitched his big wig to the devil;
Then sighing, he threw back his head,
To get a sweet drop of the bottle,
And pitiful sighing, he said:
'Oh, the hemp will be soon round my throttle,
And choke my poor windpipe to death.'

'Though sure it's the best way to die,
O! the devil a better a-livin'!
For when the gallows is high
Your journey is shorter to heaven:
But what harasses Larry the most,
And makes his poor soul melancholy,
Is that he thinks of the time when his ghost
Will come in a sheet to poor Molly;
O, sure it will kill her alive!'

So moving these last words he spoke,
We all vented our tears in a shower;
For my part, I thought my heart broke,
To see him cut down like a flower.
On his travels we watched him next day;
O! the throttler, I thought I could kill him;
But Larry not one word did say,
Nor changed till he came to King William,
Then, musha, his colour grew white.

When we came to the numbing chit,
He was tucked up so neat and so pretty,
The rumbler jogged off from his feet,
And he died with his face to the city;
He kicked, too—but that was all pride,
For soon you might see 'twas all over;
Soon after the noose was untied,
And at darkee we waked him in clover,
And sent him to take a ground sweat.

Mrs McGrath

'Oh Mrs McGrath!' the sergeant said,
'Would you like to make a soldier of your son, Ted,
With a scarlet coat and a big cocked hat,
Now Mrs McGrath, wouldn't you like that?',
    Wid yer too-ri-aa, fol-the-diddle-aa,
    Too-ri-oo-ri-oo-ri-aa,
    Wid yer too-ri-aa, fol-the diddle-aa,
    Too-ri-oo-ri-oo-ri-aa.

So Mrs McGrath lived on the sea-shore
For the space of seven long years or more,
Till she saw a big ship sailing into the bay,
'Here's my son Ted, wisha, clear the way'.

'Oh, Captain dear, where have you been,
Have you been sailing on the Mediterreen?
Or have ye any tidings of my son Ted
Is the poor boy living or is he dead?'

Then up comes Ted without any legs,
And in their place he has two wooden pegs;
She kissed him a dozen times or two,
Saying 'Holy Moses, 'tisn't you.'

'Oh then were ye drunk or were ye blind
That ye left yer two fine legs behind,
Or was it walking upon the sea
Wore yer two fine legs from the knees away?'

'Oh I wasn't drunk and I wasn't blind
But I left my two fine legs behind,
For a cannon ball on the fifth of May
Took my two fine legs from the knees away.'

'Oh then Teddy me boy,' the widow cried,
'Yer two fine legs were yer mammy's pride,
Them stumps of a tree wouldn't do at all,
Why didn't ye run from the big cannon ball?

All foreign wars I do proclaim
Between Don John and the King of Spain,
And by herrins I'll make them rue the time
That they swept the legs from a child of mine.

Oh then, if I had you back again
I'd never let ye go to fight the King of Spain,
For I'd rather my Ted as he used to be
Than the King of France and his whole Navee.'
> *Wid yer too-ri-aa, fol-the diddle-aa,*
> *Too-ri-oo-ri-oo-ri-aa,*
> *Wid yer too-ri-aa, fol-the diddle-aa,*
> *Too-ri-oo-ri-oo-ri-aa.*

Johnny, I hardly knew Ye

While going the road to sweet Athy,
   Hurroo! Hurroo!
While going the road to sweet Athy,
   Hurroo! Hurroo!

IRISH

While going the road to sweet Athy,
A stick in my hand and a drop in my eye,
A doleful damsel I heard cry:—
  'Och, Johnny, I hardly knew ye!
With drums and guns, and guns and drums,
  The enemy nearly slew ye,
  My darling dear, you look so queer,
  Och, Johnny, I hardly knew ye!

'Where are your eyes that looked so mild?
  Hurroo! Hurroo!
Where are your eyes that looked so mild?
  Hurroo! Hurroo!
Where are your eyes that looked so mild
When my poor heart you first beguiled?
Why did you run from me and the child?
  Och, Johnny, I hardly knew ye!

'Where are the legs with which you run?
  Hurroo! Hurroo!
Where are the legs with which you run?
  Hurroo! Hurroo!
Where are the legs with which you run
When you went to carry a gun?—
Indeed your dancing days are done!
  Och, Johnny, I hardly knew ye!

'It grieved my heart to see you sail,
  Hurroo! Hurroo!
It grieved my heart to see you sail,
  Hurroo! Hurroo!
It grieved my heart to see you sail
Though from my heart you took leg bail,—
Like a cod you're doubled up head and tail.
  Och, Johnny, I hardly knew ye!

'You haven't an arm and you haven't a leg,
  Hurroo! Hurroo!
You haven't an arm and you haven't a leg,
  Hurroo! Hurroo!
You haven't an arm and you haven't a leg,
You're an eyeless, noseless, chickenless egg:
You'll have to be put in a bowl to beg;
  Och, Johnny, I hardly knew ye!

'I'm happy for to see you home,
  Hurroo! Hurroo!
I'm happy for to see you home,
  Hurroo! Hurroo!
I'm happy for to see you home,
All from the island of Sulloon,
So low in flesh, so high in bone,
  Och, Johnny, I hardly knew ye!

'But sad as it is to see you so,
  Hurroo! Hurroo!
But sad as it is to see you so,
  Hurroo! Hurroo!
But sad as it is to see you so,
And to think of you now as an object of woe,
Your Peggy'll still keep ye on as her beau;
  Och, Johnny, I hardly knew ye!
With drums and guns, and guns and drums,
  The enemy nearly slew ye,
  My darling dear, you look so queer,
  Och, Johnny, I hardly knew ye!'

A Ballad of Master McGrath

Eighteen sixty nine being the date of the year,
Those Waterloo sportsmen and more did appear
For to gain the great prizes and bear them awa',
Never counting on Ireland and Master McGrath.

On the 12th of December, that day of renown,
McGrath and his keeper they left Lurgan town;
A gale in the Channel, it soon drove them o'er,
On the thirteenth they landed on fair England's shore.

And when they arrived there in big London town,
Those great English sportsmen they all gathered round—
And some of the gentlemen gave a 'Ha! Ha!'
Saying: 'Is that the great dog you call Master McGrath?'

And one of those gentlemen standing around
Says: 'I don't care a damn for your Irish greyhound';
And another he laughs with a scornful 'Ha! Ha!
We'll soon humble the pride of your Master McGrath.'

Then Lord Lurgan came forward and said: 'Gentlemen,
If there's any amongst you has money to spend—
For you nobles of England I don't care a straw—
Here's five thousand to one upon Master McGrath.'

Then McGrath he looked up and he wagged his old tail.
Informing his lordship, 'I know what you mane,
Don't fear, noble Brownlow, don't fear them, agra,
For I'll tarnish their laurels,' says Master McGrath.

And Rose stood oncovered, the great English pride,
Her master and keeper were close by her side;
They have let her away and the crowd cried, 'Hurrah!'
For the pride of all England—and Master McGrath.

As Rose and the Master they both ran along.
'Now I wonder,' says Rose, 'what took you from your home;
You should have stopped there in your Irish demesne,
And not come to gain laurels on Albion's plain,'

'Well, I know,' says McGrath, 'we have wild heather bogs,
But you'll find in old Ireland there's good men and dogs.
Lead on, bold Britannia, give none of your jaw,
Snuff that up your nostrils,' says Master McGrath.

Then the hare she went on just as swift as the wind,
He was sometime before her and sometime behind.
Rose gave the first turn according to law;
But the second was given by Master McGrath.

The hare she led on with a wonderful view,
And swift as the wind o'er the green field she flew.
But he jumped on her back and he held up his paw
'Three cheers for old Ireland,' says Master McGrath.

The Old Orange Flute

In the County Tyrone, in the town of Dungannon,
Where many a ruction myself had a han' in.
Bob Williamson lived, a weaver by trade.
And all of us thought him a stout Orange blade,
On the Twelfth of July as around it would come
Bob played on the flute to the sound of the drum,
You may talk of your harp, your piano or lute,
But there's nothing compared with the ould Orange flute.

But Bob the deceiver he took us all in,
For he married a Papish called Brigid McGinn,
Turned Papish himself, and forsook the old cause
That gave us our freedom, religion, and laws.

IRISH

Now the boys of the place made some comment upon it,
And Bob had to fly to the Province of Connacht.
He fled with his wife and his fixings to boot,
And along with the latter his old Orange flute.

At the chapel on Sundays, to atone for past deeds,
He said *Paters* and *Aves* and counted his beads,
Till after some time, at the priest's own desire,
He went with his old flute to play in the choir.
He went with his old flute to play for the Mass,
And the instrument shivered and sighed: 'Oh, alas!'
And blow as he would, though it made a great noise,
The flute would play only 'The Protestant Boys'.

Bob jumped, and he started, and got in a flutter,
And threw his old flute in the best Holy Water;
He thought that this charm would bring some other sound
When he blew it again, it played 'Croppies lie down';
And for all he could whistle, and finger, and blow,
To play Papish music he found it no go;
'Kick the Pope', 'The Boyne Water', it freely would sound,
But one Papish squeak in it couldn't be found.

At a council of priests that was held the next day,
They decided to banish the old flute away
For they couldn't knock heresy out of its head
And they bought Bob a new one to play in its stead.
So the old flute was doomed and its fate was pathetic,
'Twas fastened and burned at the stake as heretic,
While the flames roared around it they heard a strange noise—
'Twas the old flute still whistling 'The Protestant Boys'.

Kevin Barry: Died for Ireland, 1st November, 1920

In Mountjoy jail one Monday morning,
High upon the gallows tree
Kevin Barry gave his young life,
For the cause of liberty,
But a lad of eighteen summers,
Yet no one can deny
As he walked to death that morning,
He proudly held his head on high.

Just before he faced the hangman,
In his dreary prison cell,
British soldiers tortured Barry,
Just because he would not tell
The names of his brave companions,
And other things they wished to know,
'Turn informer or we'll kill you,'
Kevin Barry answered 'No'.

Calmly standing to 'attention',
While he bade his last farewell
To his broken-hearted mother,
Whose grief no one can tell.
For the cause he proudly cherished,
This sad parting had to be;
Then to death walked softly smiling,
That old Ireland might be free.

Another martyr for old Ireland,
Another murder for the crown,
Whose brutal laws may kill the Irish,
But can't keep their spirit down.

Lads like Barry are no cowards,
From the foe they will not fly,
Lads like Barry will free Ireland,
For her sake they'll live and die.

Finnegan's Wake

Tim Finnegan liv'd in Walkin Street,
A gentleman Irish mighty odd.
He had a tongue both rich and sweet,
An' to rise in the world he carried a hod,
Now Tim had a sort of a tipplin' way
With the love of the liquor he was born,
An' to help him on with his work each day,
He'd a drop of the craythur ev'ry morn.

> *Whack fol the dah, dance to your partner*
> *Welt the flure, yer trotters shake,*
> *Wasn't it the truth I told you,*
> *Lots of fun at Finnegan's Wake.*

One morning Tim was rather full,
His head felt heavy which made him shake,
He fell from the ladder and broke his skull,
So they carried him home his corpse to wake,
They rolled him up in a nice clean sheet,
And laid him out upon the bed,
With a gallon of whisky at his feet,
And a barrel of porter at his head.

His friends assembled at the wake,
And Mrs Finnegan called for lunch,
First they brought in tay and cake,
Then pipes, tobacco, and whiskey punch.

Miss Biddy O'Brien began to cry,
'Such a neat clean corpse, did you ever see,
Arrah, Tim avourneen, why did you die?'
'Ah, hould your gab,' said Paddy McGee.

Then Biddy O'Connor took up the job,
'Biddy,' says she, 'you're wrong, I'm sure,'
But Biddy gave her a belt in the gob,
And left her sprawling on the floor;
Oh, then the war did soon enrage;
'Twas woman to woman and man to man,
Shillelagh law did all engage,
And a row and a ruction soon began.

Then Mickey Maloney raised his head,
When a noggin of whiskey flew at him,
It missed and falling on the bed,
The liquor scattered over Tim;
Bedad he revives, see how he rises,
And Timothy rising from the bed,
Says, 'Whirl your liquor round like blazes,
Thanam o'n dhoul, do ye think I'm dead?'
    Whack fol the dah, dance to your partner
    Welt the flure, yer trotters shake,
    Wasn't it the truth I told you,
    Lots of fun at Finnegan's Wake.

'The Ballad of Persse O'Reilly'
JAMES JOYCE

Have you heard of one Humpty Dumpty
How he fell with a roll and a rumble
And curled up like Lord Olofa Crumple
By the butt of the Magazine Wall,
    (Chorus) Of the Magazine Wall,
            Hump, helmet and all?

He was one time our King of the Castle
Now he's kicked about like a rotten old parsnip.
And from Green Street he'll be sent by order of His Worship
To the penal jail of Mountjoy
   (Chorus) To the jail of Mountjoy!
         Jail him and joy.

He was fafafather of all schemes for to bother us
Slow coaches and immaculate contraceptives for the populace,
Mare's milk for the sick, seven dry Sundays a week,
Openair love and religion's reform,
   (Chorus) And religious reform,
         Hideous in form.

Arrah, why, says you, couldn't he manage it?
I'll go bail, my fine dairyman darling,
Like the bumping bull of the Cassidys
All your butter is in your horns.
   (Chorus) His butter is in his horns.
         Butter his horns!

(Repeat) Hurray there, Hosty, frosty Hosty, change that shirt
    on ye,
Rhyme the rann, the king of all ranns!

Balbaccio, balbuccio!
We had chaw chaw chops, chairs, chewing gum, the
    chicken-pox and china chambers
Universally provided by this soffsoaping salesman.
Small wonder He'll Cheat E'erawan our local lads nicknamed
    him
When Chimpden first took the floor
   (Chorus) With his bucketshop store
         Down Bargainweg, Lower.

IRISH

So snug was he in his hotel premises sumptuous
But soon we'll bonfire all his trash, tricks and trumpery
And 'tis short till sheriff Clancy'll be winding up his unlimited
    company
With the bailiff's bom at the door,
   (Chorus) Bimbam at the door.
           Then he'll bum no more.

Sweet bad luck on the waves washed to our island
The hooker on that hammerfast viking
And Gall's curse on the day when Eblana bay
Saw his black and tan man-o'-war.
   (Chorus) Saw his man-o'-war.
           On the harbour bar.

Where from? roars Poolbeg. Cookingha'pence, he bawls
    Donnez-moi scampitle, wick an wipin'fampiny
Fingal Mac Oscar Onesine Bargearse Boniface
Thok's min gammelhole Norveegickers moniker
Og as ay are at gammelhore Norveegickers cod.
   (Chorus) A Norwegian camel old cod.
           He is, begod.

Lift it, Hosty, lift it, ye devil ye! up with the rann, the rhyming
    rann!

It was during some fresh water garden pumping
Or, according to the *Nursing Mirror*, while admiring the
    monkeys
That our heavyweight heathen Humpharey
Made bold a maid to woo
   (Chorus) Woohoo, what'll she doo!
           The general lost her maidenloo!

IRISH

He ought to blush for himself, the old hayheaded philosopher,
For to go and shove himself that way on top of her.
Begob, he's the crux of the catalogue
Of our antediluvial zoo,
   (Chorus) Messrs. Billing and Coo.
        Noah's larks, good as noo.

He was joulting by Wellington's monument
Our rotorious hippopopotamuns
When some bugger let down the backstrap of the omnibus
And he caught his death of fusiliers,
   (Chorus) With his rent in his rears.
        Give him six years.

'Tis sore pity for his innocent poor children
But look out for his missus legitimate!
When that frew gets a grip of old Earwicker
Won't there be earwigs on the green?
   (Chorus) Big earwigs on the green,
        The largest ever you seen.

Suffoclose! Shikespower! Seudodanto! Anonymoses!

Then we'll have a free trade Gael's band and mass meeting
For to sod the brave son of Scandiknavery.
And we'll bury him down in Oxmantown
Along with the devil and Danes,
   (Chorus) With the deaf and dumb Danes,
        And all their remains.

And not all the king's men nor his horses
Will resurrect his corpus
For there's no true spell in Connacht or hell
   (Bis) That's able to raise a Cain.

Van Diemen's Land

Come all you gallant poachers that ramble void of care,
That walk out on a moonlight night with your dog and gun and
　　　　　snare.
The hare and lofty pheasant you have at your command,
Not thinking of your last career upon Van Diemen's Land.

Poor Thomas Brown from Nenagh town, Jack Murphy and
　　　　　poor Joe
Were three determined poachers as the country well does know
By the keepers of the land, my boys, one night they were
　　　　　trepanned
And for fourteen years transported unto Van Diemen's Land.

The first day that we landed upon that fatal shore
The planters came around us, there might be twenty score.
They ranked us off like horses and they sold us out of hand
And they yoked us to the plough, brave boys, to plough Van
　　　　　Diemen's Land.

The cottages we live in are built with sods of clay
We have rotten straw for bedding but we dare not say nay.
Our cots we fence with firing and slumber when we can
To keep the wolves and tigers from us in Van Diemen's Land.

Oft times when I do slumber I have a pleasant dream
With my sweet girl sitting near me close by a purling stream;
I am roaming through old Ireland with my true love by the
　　　　　hand,
But awaken broken-hearted upon Van Diemen's Land.

IRISH

God bless our wives and families, likewise that happy shore,
That isle of sweet contentment which we shall ne'er see more;
As for the wretched families see them we seldom can;
There are twenty men for one woman in Van Diemen's Land.

There was a girl from Nenagh town, Peg Brophy was her name,
For fourteen years transported was, we all well knew the same;
But our planter bought her freedom and married her out of
                                        hand
And she gives to us good usage upon Van Dièmen's Land.

But fourteen years is a long time, that is our fatal doom,
For nothing else but poaching for that is all we done;
You would leave off both dog and gun and poaching every man
If you but knew the hardship that's in Van Diemen's Land.

Oh, if I had a thousand pounds all laid out in my hand,
I'd give it all for liberty if that I could command,
Again to Ireland I'd return and be a happy man
And bid adieu to poaching and to Van Diemen's Land.

VII

Australian and American

The Wild Colonial Boy

'Tis of a wild Colonial boy, Jack Doolan was his name,
Of poor but honest parents he was born in Castlemaine.
He was his father's only hope, his mother's only joy,
And dearly did his parents love the wild Colonial boy.

Chorus: Come, all my hearties, we'll roam the mountains high,
Together we will plunder, together we will die.
We'll wander over valleys, and gallop over plains,
And we'll scorn to live in slavery, bound down with iron
chains.

He was scarcely sixteen years of age when he left his father's
home,
And through Australia's sunny clime a bushranger did roam.
He robbed those wealthy squatters, their stock he did destroy,
And a terror to Australia was the wild Colonial boy.

In sixty-one this daring youth commenced his wild career,
With a heart that knew no danger, no foeman did he fear.
He stuck up the Beechworth mail-coach, and robbed Judge
MacEvoy,
Who trembled, and gave up his gold to the wild Colonial boy.

He bade the judge 'Good morning', and told him to beware,
That he'd never rob a hearty chap that acted on the square,
And never to rob a mother of her son and only joy,
Or else you may turn outlaw, like the wild Colonial boy.

One day as he was riding the mountain-side along,
A-listening to the little birds, their pleasant laughing song,
Three mounted troopers rode along—Kelly, Davis, and
FitzRoy—
They thought that they would capture him, the wild Colonial
boy.

229

'Surrender now, Jack Doolan, you see there's three to one.
Surrender now, Jack Doolan, you daring highwayman.'
He drew a pistol from his belt, and shook the little toy.
'I'll fight, but not surrender,' said the wild Colonial boy.

He fired at Trooper Kelly and brought him to the ground,
And in return from Davis received a mortal wound.
All shattered through the jaws he lay still firing at FitzRoy,
And that's the way they captured him—the wild Colonial boy.

The Death of Morgan

Throughout Australian history no tongue or pen can tell
Of such preconcerted treachery—there is no parallel—
As the tragic deed of Morgan's death; without warning he was
  shot
On Peechelba station, it will never be forgot.

I have oft-times heard of murders in Australia's golden land,
But such an open daylight scene of thirty in a band,
Assembled at the dawn of day, and then to separate,
Behind the trees, some on their knees, awaiting Morgan's fate.

Too busy was the servant-maid; she trotted half the night
From Macpherson's down to Rutherford's the tidings to recite.
A messenger was sent away who for his neck had no regard,
He returned with a troop of traps in hopes of their reward.

But they were all disappointed; McQuinlan was the man
Who fired from his rifle and shot rebellious Dan.
Concealed he stood behind a tree till his victim came in view,
And as Morgan passed his doom was cast—the unhappy man
  he slew.

There was a rush for trophies, soon as the man was dead;
They cut off his beard, his ears, and the hair from off his head.
In truth it was a hideous sight as he struggled on the ground,
They tore the clothes from off his back and exposed the fatal
    wound.

Oh, Morgan was the travellers' friend; the squatters all rejoice
That the outlaw's life is at an end, no more they'll hear his voice.
Success attend all highwaymen who do the poor some good;
But my curse attend a treacherous man who'd shed another's
    blood.

Farewell to Burke, O'Meally, Young Gilbert and Ben Hall,
Likewise to Daniel Morgan, who fell by rifle-ball;
So all young men be warned and never take up arms,
Remember this, how true it is, bushranging hath no charms!

The Banks of the Condamine

Oh, hark the dogs are barking, love,
I can no longer stay.
The men are all gone mustering
And it is nearly day.
And I must off by the morning light
Before the sun doth shine,
To meet the Sydney shearers
On the banks of the Condamine.

Oh Willie, dearest Willie,
I'll go along with you,
I'll cut off all my auburn fringe
And be a shearer, too,
I'll cook and count your tally, love,
While ringer-o you shine,
And I'll wash your greasy moleskins
On the banks of the Condamine.

Oh, Nancy, dearest Nancy,
With me you cannot go,
The squatters have given orders, love,
No woman should do so;
Your delicate constitution
Is not equal unto mine,
To stand the constant tigering,
On the banks of the Condamine.

Oh Willie, dearest Willie,
Then stay back home with me,
We'll take up a selection
And a farmer's wife I'll be:
I'll help you husk the corn, love,
And cook your meals so fine
You'll forget the ram-stag mutton
On the banks of the Condamine.

Oh, Nancy, dearest Nancy,
Please do not hold me back,
Down there the boys are waiting,
And I must be on the track;
So here's a good-bye kiss, love,
Back home here I'll incline
When we've shore the last of the jumbucks
On the banks of the Condamine.

The New-Chum's First Trip

Now if you will listen I'll tell you a story,
Concerning some drovers a few months ago,
They started away from the Maranoa River
With five hundred store-bullocks to the Logan to go.

AUSTRALIAN AND AMERICAN

I heard many stories about the life of a drover,
His fancy whip-handle, and jingling quart-pot,
And smoking and yarning at night round the campfire,
Some people will say, 'What a life he has got.'

But the gay drover's life is not always sunshine,
No doubt some old hands will tell you the same,
You are roused out of bed about two in the morning,
To keep watch on those cattle, lest it thunder or rain.

The dingoes are howling, the thunder is growling,
The night is pitch dark as we start to retire,
The night-watch is singing, horse-bells are ringing,
And breakfast next morn by the light of the fire.

How well I remember the day at Taroom,
When we crossed o'er the Dawson amid pouring rain,
And on past the Auburn, no flour or tobacco,
I wished I was back in old Mitchell again.

Then on past Boondoomba and Burandowan station,
Tobacco it seemed was a thing of the past,
Night-watching is dreary, horses footsore and weary,
The ground wet and boggy, and the creek rising fast.

I remember Taabinga, a nice pretty station,
And swimming the cattle across Barker Creek,
And the night at Nanango, our blankets were soaking,
The rain fell in torrents, and the tent it did leak.

Then on past Nanango, and Taromeo station
The road rough and stony, some bullocks were lame,
The storm-birds are calling, the rain is still falling,
We crossed over a range, I've forgotten its name.

Then down in the Valley, the feed is much better,
We camped in Bob Williams's paddock that night,
Salt beef and burnt damper, and tea without sugar,
Our clothes wet and sodden, a pitiful sight.

On then past Esk and on to Tarampa,
The rain it has cleared, the day's fairly fine,
Our spirits are lighter, the night is much brighter;
At Grandchaster station we crossed the rail line.

Now our trip is near over, the cattle in clover,
The weather has cleared and our blankets are dry,
The days are quite breezy, and the going is easy,
We camped out that night 'neath a clear starry sky.

Next day with elation we reached Bromelton station,
We delivered the cattle with many a curse,
Our long trip was over, but said the boss drover,
'It was a pretty rough trip, but it could have been worse.'

Stir the Wallaby Stew

Poor Dad he got five years or more as everybody knows,
And now he lives in Maitland Jail with broad arrows on his
  clothes,
He branded all of Brown's clean-skins and never left a tail,
So I'll relate the family's woes since Dad got put in jail.

Chorus: So stir the wallaby stew,
      Make soup of the kangaroo tail,
      I tell you things is pretty tough
      Since Dad got put in jail.

Our sheep were dead a month ago, not rot but blooming fluke,
Our cow was boozed last Christmas Day by my big brother Luke,
And Mother has a shearer cove for ever within hail,
The family will have grown a bit since Dad got put in jail.

Our Bess got shook upon a bloke, he's gone we don't know
    where,
He used to act about the shed, but he ain't acted square;
I've sold the buggy on my own, the place is up for sale,
That won't be all that isn't junked when Dad comes out of jail.

They let Dad out before his time, to give us a surprise.
He came and slowly looked around, and gently blessed our eyes,
He shook hands with the shearer cove and said he thought
    things stale,
So left him here to shepherd us and battled back to jail.

Barbara Allen

Down in London where I was raised,
    Down where I got my learning,
I fell in love with a pretty little girl;
    Her name was Barbara Ellen.

He courted her for seven long years,
    She said she would not have him.
Pretty William went home and took down sick
    And sent for Barbara Ellen.

He wrote her a letter on his death-bed;
    He wrote it slow and moving.
Go take this to my pretty little love,
    And tell her I am dying.

They took it to his pretty little love,
    She read it slow and mourning.
Go take this to my pretty little love,
    And tell him I am coming.

As she walked on to his bed-side,
   Says: Young man, young man, you're dying.
He turned his pale face toward the wall
   And bursted out a-crying.

He reached his lily-white hand to her.
   O come and tell me 'howdey'.
O no, O no, O no, says she,
   And she would not go about him.

Do you remember last Saturday night
   Down at my father's dwelling?
You passed the drink to the ladies all around
   And slighted Barbara Ellen.

Yes, I remember last Saturday night
   Down at your father's dwelling,
I passed the drink to the ladies all around,
   My heart to Barbara Ellen.

As she walked down those long stair-steps,
   She heard some death-bells ringing,
And every bell it seemed to say:
   Hard-hearted Barbara Ellen,
   Hard-hearted Barbara Ellen.

As she walked down that shady grove,
   She heard some birds a-singing,
And every bird it seemed to say,
   Hard-hearted Barbara Ellen,
   Hard-hearted Barbara Ellen.

As she walked out the very next day,
   She saw his corpse a-coming.
O lay him down, O lay him down,
   And let me look upon him.

The more she looked the worse she felt,
    Till she bursted out a-crying:
I once could have saved pretty William's life,
    But I would not go about him.

O mother, O mother, go make my bed,
    Go make it soft and narrow;
Pretty William has died for pure, pure love,
    And I shall die for sorrow.

O father, O father, go dig my grave,
    Go dig it deep and narrow;
Pretty William has died for me today,
    And I shall die tomorrow.

A rose grew up from William's grave,
    From Barbara Ellen's a brier.
They grew and they grew to the top of the church-house
    Till they could not grow any higher.

They grew and they grew to the top of the church-house
    Till they could not grow any higher,
And there they tied in a true love's knot,
    And the rose wrapped round the brier.

The Wild Rippling Water

As I was out walkin' an' a-ramblin' one day,
I spied a fair couple a-makin' their way;
One was a lady and a fair one was she,
An' the other a cowboy, an' a brave one were he.

Says, 'Where are you goin', my pretty fair maid?'
'Jest down by the river, jest down by the shade,
Jest down by the river, jest down by the spring,
See the wild ripplin' water an' hear the nightingale sing.'

They hadn't been there but an hour or so,
Till he drew from his satchel a fiddle and bow;
He tuned his fiddle all on the high string
An' he played this tune over an' over again.

'Now', said the cowboy, 'I should have been gone.'
'No, no,' said the pretty maid, 'jest play one more song.
I'd rather hear the fiddle played on that one string
As to see the water glide an' hear the nightingale sing.'

He tuned up his fiddle and he rosined his bow;
He played her a lecture, he played it all o'er;
He played her a lecture that made the valley ring.
'Hark! Hark!' said the fair maid. 'Hear the nightingale sing.'

She said, 'Dear cowboy, will you marry me?'
He said: 'Dear lady, that could never be.
I have a wife in Arizona, an' a lady is she;
One wife on a cow-ranch is plenty for me.

'I'll go to Mexico, I'll stay there one year;
I'll drink sweet wine an' I'll drink lots of beer.
If I ever return, it will be in the spring,
To see the bright ripplin' water, hear the nightingale sing.'

'Come all you young maidens, take warning from me;
Never place your affections in a cowboy too free;
He'll go away an' leave you like mine did me;
Leave you to rock cradles, sing 'Bye-o-babee.'

Sweet Betsy from Pike

Did you ever hear tell of Sweet Betsy from Pike,
Who crossed the wide mountains with her lover Ike,
With two yoke of cattle and one spotted hog,
A tall Shanghai rooster and an old yellow dog.

Chorus:
Hoodle dang fol-de di-do, hoodle dang fol-de day.

They swam the wide rivers and climbed the tall peaks
And camped on the prairies for weeks upon weeks,
Starvation and cholera, hard work and slaughter,
They reached California spite of hell and high water.

The Injuns come down in a wild yelling horde
And Betsy got skeered they would scalp her adored,
So behind the front wagon-wheel Betsy did crawl,
And fought off the Injuns with musket and ball.

They camped on the prairie one bright, starry night,
They broke out the whisky and Betsy got tight,
She sang and she shouted and romped o'er the plain,
And showed her bare bum to the whole wagon train.

The wagon tipped over with a terrible crash,
And out on the prairie rolled all sorts of trash,
A few little baby clothes, done up with care,
Looked rather suspicious, but 'twas all on the square.

Sweet Betsy got up with a great deal of pain
And declared she'd go back to Pike County again,
Then Ike heaved a sigh and they fondly embraced,
And she travelled along with his arm round her waist.

They passed the Sierras through mountains of snow,
Till old California was sighted below.
Sweet Betsy she hollered, and Ike gave a cheer,
Saying 'Betsy, my darlin', I'm a made millioneer.'

A miner said, 'Betsy, will you dance with me?'
'I will that, old hoss, if you don't make too free.
But don't dance me hard, do you want to know why?
Doggon ye, I'm chock full of strong alkali.'

Long Ike and Sweet Betsy got married, of course,
But Ike, who was jealous, obtained a divorce,
And Betsy, well satisfied, said with a smile,
'I've six good men waitin' within half a mile.'

The Jam on Gerry's Rock

Come all ye true born shanty-boys, whoever that ye be,
I would have you pay attention and listen unto me,
Concerning a young shanty-boy so tall, genteel and brave.
'Twas on a jam on Gerry's Rocks he met a wat'ry grave.

It happened on a Sunday morn as you shall quickly hear,
Our logs were piled up mountain high, there being no one to
    keep them clear.
Our boss he cried, 'Turn out, brave boys. Your hearts are void
    of fear.
We'll break that jam on Gerry's Rocks, and for Agonstown
    we'll steer.'

Some of them were willing enough, but others they hung back.
'Twas for to work on Sabbath they did not think 'twas right.
But six of our brave Canadian boys did volunteer to go
And break the jam on Gerry's Rocks with their foreman,
    young Monroe.

They had not rolled off many logs when the boss to them did
   say,
'I'd have you be on your guard, brave boys. That jam will soon
   give way.'
But scarce the warning had he spoke when the jam did break
   and go,
And it carried away these six brave youths and their foreman,
   young Monroe.

When the rest of the shanty-boys these sad tidings came to
   hear,
To search for their dead comrades to the river they did steer.
One of these a headless body found, to their sad grief and woe,
Lay cut and mangled on the beach the head of young Monroe.

They took him from the water and smoothed down his raven
   hair.
There was one fair form amongst them, her cries would rend the
   air.
There was one fair form amongst them, a maid from Saginaw
   town.
Her sighs and cries would rend the skies for her lover that was
   drowned.

They buried him quite decently, being on the seventh of May.
Come all the rest of you shanty-boys, for your dead comrade
   pray.
'Tis engraved on a little hemlock tree that at his head doth
   grow,
The name, the date, and the drowning of this hero, young
   Monroe.

Miss Clara was a noble girl, likewise the raftsman's friend.
Her mother was a widow woman lived at the river's bend.
The wages of her own true love the boss to her did pay,
And a liberal subscription she received from the shanty-boys
   next day.

Miss Clara did not long survive her great misery and grief.
In less than three months afterwards death came to her relief.
In less than three months afterwards she was called to go,
And her last request was granted—to be laid by young Monroe.

Come all the rest of ye shanty-men who would like to go and
    see,
On a little mound by the river's bank there stands a hemlock
    tree.
The shanty-boys cut the woods all round. These lovers they lie
    low.
Here lies Miss Clara Dennison and her shanty-boy, Monroe.

The Dying Cowboy

As I rode out by Tom Sherman's bar-room,
As I rode out so early one day,
'Twas there I espied a handsome young cowboy,
All dressed in white linen, all clothed for the grave.

'I see by your outfit that you are a cowboy,'
These words he did say as I boldly stepped by.
'Come sit down beside me and hear my sad story,
For I'm shot in the breast and I know I must die.

'Then beat your drum slowly and play your fife lowly,
And play the dead march as you carry me along,
And take me to the graveyard and throw the sod o'er me,
For I'm a young cowboy and I know I've done wrong.

'"Twas once in the saddle I used to go dashing,
'Twas once in the saddle I used to go gay,
But I first took to drinking and then to card-playing,
Got shot in the body and I'm dying today.

'Let sixteen gamblers come handle my coffin,
Let sixteen young cowboys come sing me a song,
Take me to the green valley and lay the sod o'er me,
For I'm a poor cowboy and I know I've done wrong.

'Go bring me back a cup of cool water
To cool my parched lips,' this cowboy then said.
Before I returned, his soul had departed
And gone to his Maker—the cowboy lay dead.

We swung our ropes slowly and rattled our spurs lowly,
And gave a wild whoop as we carried him on,
For we all loved our comrade, so brave, young and handsome,
We all loved our comrade, although he'd done wrong.

John Henry

John Henry was a lil baby,
Sittin' on his mama's knee,
Said: 'De Big Bend Tunnel on de C. & O. road
Gonna cause de death of me,
Lawd, lawd, gonna cause de death of me.'

Cap'n says to John Henry,
'Gonna bring me a steam drill 'round,
Gonna take dat steam drill out on de job,
Gonna whop dat steel on down,
Lawd, lawd, gonna whop dat steel on down.'

John Henry tol' his cap'n,
Lightnin' was in his eye:
'Cap'n, bet yo' las' red cent on me,
Fo' I'll beat it to de bottom or I'll die,
Lawd, lawd, I'll beat it to de bottom or I'll die.'

Sun shine hot an' burnin',
Wer'n't no breeze a-tall,
Sweat ran down like water down a hill,
Dat day John Henry let his hammer fall,
Lawd, lawd, dat day John Henry let his hammer fall.

John Henry went to de tunnel,
An' dey put him in de lead to drive,
De rock so tall an' John Henry so small,
Dat he lied down his hammer an' he cried,
Lawd, lawd, dat he lied down his hammer an' he cried.

John Henry started on de right hand,
De steam drill started on de lef'—
'Before I'd let dis steam drill beat me down,
I'd hammer my fool self to death,
Lawd, lawd, I'd hammer my fool self to death.'

White man tol' John Henry,
'Nigger, damn yo' soul,
You might beat dis steam an' drill of mine,
When de rocks in dis mountain turn to gol',
Lawd, lawd, when de rocks in dis mountain turn to gol'.'

John Henry said to his shaker,
'Nigger, why don' you sing?
I'm throwin' twelve poun's from my hips on down,
Jes' listen to de col' steel ring,
Lawd, lawd, jes' listen to de col' steel ring.'

Oh, de captain said to John Henry,
'I b'lieve this mountain's sinkin' in.'
John Henry said to his captain, oh my!
'Ain' nothin' but my hammer suckin' win',
Lawd, lawd, ain' nothin' but my hammer suckin' win'.'

John Henry tol' his shaker,
'Shaker, you better pray,
For if I miss dis six-foot steel,
Tomorrow'll be yo' buryin' day,
Lawd, lawd, tomorrow'll be yo' buryin' day.'

John Henry tol' his captain,
'Look yonder what I see—
Yo' drill's done broke an' yo' hole's done choke,
An' you cain' drive steel like me,
Lawd, lawd, an' you cain' drive steel like me.'

De man dat invented de steam drill,
Thought he was mighty fine.
John Henry drove his fifteen feet,
An' de steam drill only made nine,
Lawd, lawd, an' de steam drill only made nine.

De hammer dat John Henry swung,
It weighed over nine pound;
He broke a rib in his lef'-han' side,
An' his intrels fell on de groun',
Lawd, lawd, an' his intrels fell on de groun'.

All de womens in de Wes',
When dey heared of John Henry's death,
Stood in de rain, flagged de eas'-boun' train,
Goin' where John Henry fell dead,
Lawd, lawd, goin' where John Henry fell dead.

John Henry's lil mother,
She was all dressed in red,
She jumped in bed, covered up her head,
Said she didn' know her son was dead,
Lawd, lawd, didn' know her son was dead.

Dey took John Henry to de graveyard,
An' dey buried him in de san',
An' every locomotive come roarin' by,
Says, 'Dere lays a steel-drivin' man,
Lawd, lawd, dere lays a steel-drivin' man.'

John Hardy

John Hardy was standing in the gambling room door,
He was not concerned in the game.
Up stepped his little woman, threw down fifty cents,
Says, 'Count John Hardy in the game.'
Lord, Lord, says, 'Count John Hardy in the game.'

John Hardy picked up his fifty cents,
Says, 'Half of this I'll play.
The man that wins my fifty cents,
Shoot him down and leave him lay.'
Lord, Lord! 'Shoot him down and leave him lay.'

John Hardy lost his fifty cents;
Was all he had in the game.
He drew a forty-four from his side,
Blowed out that poor negro's brains,
Lord, Lord! blowed out that poor negro's brains.

John Hardy had ten miles to go,
And half of that he run;
He ran till he came to the broad river bank.
He fell to his breast and swum.
Lord, Lord! he fell to his breast and swum.

John Hardy was lying on the broad river bank,
As drunk as a man could be.
Up stepped John Gamel and another police,
Says, 'John, come go with me,
John Hardy, come go with me.'

They took John Hardy to have his trial.
No one would go his bail.
His father and mother was standing by
When they locked John Hardy up in jail,
Lord, Lord! when they locked John Hardy up in jail.

John Hardy had but one little girl;
He kept her dressed in red.
And when she saw her papa through the cold iron bars
Says, 'Mama, I had rather see him dead.'
Lord, Lord! says, 'Mama, I had rather see him dead.'

'Oh, when I die don't bury me at all,
Put me down in a silver gum.
Sing the songs my father used to sing,
With a big brass horn blow on.
Blow on! with a big brass horn blow on.'

The last time I saw John Hardy's face
He was standing on a scaffold high.
The last word I heard John Hardy say
Was 'I want to go to heaven when I die.'
Lord, Lord! was 'I want to go to heaven when I die.'

Blow the Candle Out

It was late last Saturday evening
I went to see my dear,
The candles were all burning
And the moon shone bright and clear.
I rapped on her window
To ease her of her pain,
She rose and let me in
And then barred the door again.

I like well your behaviour
And this I often say—
I cannot rest contented
While you are far away;
But the roads they are so muddy
I cannot roam about,
So roll me in your arms, love,
And blow the candle out.

Your father and your mother
In yonder room do lie,
A-huggin' one another
So why not you and I?
A-huggin' one another,
Without a fear or doubt
So roll me in your arms, love,
And blow the candle out.

And if we prove successful, love,
Please name it after me,
Hug it neat and kiss it sweet
And dap it on your knee.
When my three years are ended
And my time it is run out,
Then I will prove my indebtedness
By blowing the candle out.

Notes

25. *Riddles Wisely Expounded*. Child 1C (Motherwell's MS, 1820 and after)
One of the many riddle-stories found in folk-lore, based on the magical power of the Word, which is here used to outwit a supernatural adversary.
speird: asked.

26. *The Elfin Knight*. Child 2A (Broadside *c*. 1670)
A common motif in folk-lore: a girl wins a husband by quickness of wit.
kist: chest. *eare*: plough. *bigg*: build.

28. *Lady Isabel and the Elf-Knight*. Child 4 (Motherwell's MS)
This ballad is found all over Europe; the best version is the Dutch 'Halewijn'.
gowan: daisy. *ban*: bound.

29. *Earl Brand* (*The Douglas Tragedy*). Child 7 (Motherwell's MS)
A close parallel with the Danish ballad 'Ribold and Guldborg', and probably ultimately from ancient Germanic epic (Hildesaga).
scad: reflection.

32. *The Twa Sisters*. Child 10B (Jamieson-Brown MS, 1783–1801)
jaw: wave. *wardles make*: earthly mate.

34. *Lord Randal*. Child 12A (Macmath MS, mid 19th century)
Early nineteenth century; there is a parallel in Italian, 'L'Avvelenato', from the seventeenth, but the story may go back to Ranulf, Earl of Chester, mentioned as a subject of ballads by Langland in the late fourteenth century (see Introduction).

36. *The Cruel Mother.* Child 20B (Johnson's *Scots Musical Museum*, 1787–1803)

twinnd: deprived.

37. *The Three Ravens.* Child 26 (*Melismata*, 1611)

An archaic ballad with parallel themes in Danish balladry. The fallow doe probably comes from medieval romance, and before that from Celtic legend.

lake: pit. *leman*: lover.

38. *The Twa Corbies.* Scott's *Minstrelsy of the Scottish Border*, 1802–03

'Communicated by C. K. Sharpe "as written down from a tradition by a lady" '. Probably a literary reworking of 'The Three Ravens'.

corbie: carrion-crow. *hause-bane*: neck bone.

38. *Corpus Christi.* R. L. Greene, *The Early English Carol* (MS of Richard Hill, *c.* 1500)

A fifteenth century carol, which may be the origin of 'The Three Ravens', as B. H. Bronson suggests, or may have a common source.

mak: mate.

39. *Clerk Colvill.* Child 42B (Herd, *The Ancient and Modern Scots Songs*, 1769, with interpolated lines from Willliam Tytler's Brown MS, 1783; first published by A. B. Friedman, *Viking Book of Folk Ballads.*)

Scandinavian parallels make it clear that the mermaid was Colvill's first love, and is taking her revenge.

speer: ask. *gare*: strip of cloth.

41. *Young Beichan* (*Lord Bateman*). Child 53A (Jamieson-Brown MS, 1783–1801)

A common motif in European balladry and medieval romance.

44. *Fair Annie.* Child 62A (Scott's *Minstrelsy*)

Probably derived from the twelfth century 'Lai del Fresne' (Lay of the Ash) by Marie de France, or from a common source.

jimp: slender.

NOTES

49. *Child Waters.* Child 63A (Percy Folio MS, 17th century)
Fifteenth century minstrel ballad.
worldlye make: earthly mate.

54. *Young Hunting.* Child 68 (Campbell and Sharp, *Appalachians*, Vol. I, p. 101)
Twentieth century American version of a ballad known in eighteenth century Scotland, with perhaps earlier Danish parallels.

56. *Clerk Saunders.* Child 69 (Motherwell's MS, and Herd's MSS, following the version given by A. B. Friedman in the *Viking Book of Folk Ballads*)
The first published version was in Scott's *Minstrelsy*; the ballad may be a composite.

58. *The Wife of Usher's Well.* Child 79A (Scott's *Minstrelsy*)
carline: peasant. *fashes*: storms. *birk*: birch. *syke*: brook. *sheugh*: ditch. *channerin*: gnawing.
It is said that birch is a charm for ghosts to keep off the living; but the folk-lore of this moving poem need not be taken too seriously. It may be yet another Scots creation of the eighteenth century.

60. *Little Musgrave and Lady Barnard.* Child 81A (*Wit Restor'd*, 1658)
A broadside-type version of a Northern folk ballad.
wax so wood: go so mad.

64. *Lamkin.* Child 93A (Jamieson, *Popular Ballads and Songs*, 1806)

67. *The Bailiff's Daughter of Islington.* Child 105 (seventeenth century broadsides)

69. *The Great Silkie of Sule Skerry.* Child 113 (*Proceedings, Society of Antiquaries of Scotland*, 1852)
Sule Skerry is a small island in the Orkneys; a silkie is a seal. There are many legends about the half-human nature of seals in Orcadian, Highland and Irish folk-lore.

lily wean: little child. *grumly*: fierce. *aught a bairn to me*: had a child by me.

70. *Sir Hugh* (*The Jew's Daughter*). Child 155A (Jamieson, *Popular Ballads and Songs*)

Based on the legend of Hugh of Lincoln, one of the stories of ritual murder that were circulated by the medieval monastic writers; another appears in Chaucer's 'Prioresses Tale'.
wyle: deceive.

72. *The Gypsy Laddie*. Child 200B (C. K. Sharpe's MSS, early 19th century)

Other versions call the gypsy Johnny Faa, which was a common family name among the Romany folk of the sixteenth and seventeenth centuries.
glamourie: magic. *hinny*: honey.

75. *James Harris* (*The Demon Lover*). Child 243F (Scott's *Minstrelsy*)

There is a seventeenth century broadside version.
drumly: gloomy.

77. *Get up and Bar the Door*. Child 275A (Herd, *The Ancient and Modern Scots Songs*, 1769)

Based on a fabliau or comic folk-tale.

81. *Robin Hood and the Monk*. Child 119 (MS of about 1450, Cambridge University Library)

One of the earliest ballads, and of the minstrel kind.
sheyne: beautiful. *on tre*: on the Cross. *mylner sun*: miller's son.
wyght: sturdy. *slon*: slain. *lyne*: lime tree. *holde*: wager.
buske and brome: bush and broom. *ferly*: wondrous.
lyed: called a liar. *by hit*: pay for it. *layne*: lie. *rode*: Cross.
spar: shut. *buske and bowne*: make ready. *long of the*: thy fault.
radly: quickly. *yare*: ready. *throly*: doggedly. *thrast*: pressed.
wone: number. *rule*: weeping. *tristil-tre*: tree of tryst.
emys: uncle's. *at a high stage*: from the upper floor.

hende: kindly. *spyrred*: asked. *lyng*: grass. *infere*: together.
so mot I the: so may I thrive. *dere*: harm. *warison*: reward.
grith: pardon. *i-wysse*: indeed.

94. *Robin Hood's Death.* Child 120B (*The English Archer*,
     Paisley, printed by John Neilson for George Caldwell near
     the Cross, 1786)

96. *Chevy Chase (Hunting of the Cheviot).* Child 162B (seven-
     teenth century broadsides)

There is a fuller version in the Percy MS, going back to the
sixteenth or fifteenth century. It is a minstrel's ballad, about
the same event as the Battle of Otterburn (Child 161): this took
place in 1388.

106. *Johnie Armstrong.* Child 169A (*Wit Restor'd*, 1658)

The Armstrongs of Liddesdale were prominent in border forays
in the early sixteenth century.

108. *Johnie Cock.* Child 114A (Percy Papers, communicated to
      Percy by Miss Fisher of Carlisle, 1780)

Possibly 'traditional' rather than 'Border'.

111. *Captain Car (Edom o' Gordon).* Child 178 (1755, version
      supplied by Sir David Dalrymple)

Another version dates from the late sixteenth century; it
describes the burning of Towrie castle, Aberdeenshire, by
Adam Gordon and Captain Ker in 1571, during the religious
conflicts.

hald: stronghold. *drie*: endure. *wae worth*: woe befall.
ground-wa-stane: foundation stone. *jimp*: slender.
towd: let down. *busk and boon*: get ready. *freits*: omens.
mudie: bold. *lemanless*: loverless.

119. *Edward.* Child 13B (Percy's *Reliques*, 1765, communicated
      by Sir David Dalrymple)

A literary version of a genuine traditional ballad, known in
Scandinavia.

121. *Sir Patrick Spens.* Child 58A (Percy's *Reliques*, 1765,
      'given from two MS copies, transmitted from Scotland'.)

There are several other Scottish versions of later date, but the ballad does not seem to come from folk tradition, nor can the event be proved to be historical. Perhaps a literary composition of the eighteenth century.

122. *Lord Thomas and Fair Annet*. Child 73A (Percy's *Reliques*, 1765, 'given, with some corrections, from a MS copy transmitted from Scotland'.)
A genuine traditional ballad, found also in seventeenth century broadsides; but the Percy version differs from the others both in incidents and in literary skill.

127. *Thomas Rymer*. Child 37A (Jamieson)
Based on the medieval romance of Thomas of Erceldoune, whose reputation as prophet and poet dates from the fourteenth century.

129. *Tam Lin*. Child 39A (Johnson's *Scots Musical Museum*, 1792, communicated by Robert Burns)
The motifs connected with the supernatural lover are archaic, and the ballad probably dates from the sixteenth century; but this version shows some literary reshaping.

135. *Geordie*. Child 209A (Johnson's *Scots Musical Museum*, 1792, communicated by Robert Burns)
The story is probably concerned with George Gordon, fourth Earl of Huntly, and is set in sixteenth century Aberdeenshire.

138. *Marie Hamilton*. Child 173A (Sharpe's *Ballad Book*, 1824)
There does not seem to be a historical source for the story in the reign of Mary Stuart; and the resemblance to the story of a Miss Hamilton at the court of Peter the Great of Russia may be accidental. Possibly an eighteenth century invention.

143. *O Waly, Waly*. Child 204 (Ramsay's *Tea-Table Miscellany*, 1750)
Other versions called 'Jamie Douglas', or a variant, give this lament an historical setting: Lady Barbara Erskine

was separated from James, second Marquis of Douglas, in 1681.

144. *The Bonny Earl of Murray.* Child 181A (Ramsay's *Tea-Table Miscellany*, 1750)

James, Earl of Murray, was killed by the Earl of Huntly in 1592.

145. *Bonny George Campbell.* Child 210C (Smith's *Scotish Minstrel*, 1820–24)

George or James Campbell cannot be identified; this is a lament perhaps influenced by the Highland *coronach*.

146. *The Unquiet Grave.* Child 78 (Cecil Sharp, *One Hundred English Folksongs*, Novello, 1916)

Many versions known in southern England.

147. *Still Growing.* Journal of the Folk Song Society, II, p. 44.

Not accepted by Child, but widespread in Southern England and also found in Ireland. It has been suggested that it was originally Scottish; and that the boy was the young Lord Craigton, who married the daughter of his guardian, Sir Robert Innes, in 1631 and died in 1634.

148. *The Grey Cock.* Cf. Child 248 (Campbell and Sharp, *Appalachians*, I, 159)

Descended from the medieval *aubade*, the lovers' song of parting at dawn.

line 1, the fever, possibly for 'Phoebus'.

149. *The Streams of Lovely Nancy.* Journal of the Folk Song Society, VII, p. 59 (copyright 1923); amended text in The Penguin Book of English Folk Songs, ed. R. Vaughan Williams and A. L. Lloyd, 1959.

The meaning is obscure; for a discussion, see M. J. C. Hodgart, *The Ballads*, 1950, p. 168.

150. *Six Dukes went a-fishing.* Journal of the Folk Song Society, III, p. 170. Miss Broadwood thinks it may refer to William de la Pole, first Duke of Suffolk who was murdered in 1450, and his body cast on the shore. The folk-

song has something in common with a broadside of 1690, 'The Noble Funeral of the Renowned Champion the Duke of Grafton . . .'

151. *The Cherry-Tree Carol.* Child 54A (Sandys, *Christmas Carols*, 1833)

Widespread in Southern and Western England; based on the New Testament Apocrypha (Pseudo-Matthew).

152. *The Bitter Withy.* (Printed by F. Sidgwick in *Notes and Queries*, 29th July, 1905)

Not in Child; a similar ballad is called 'The Holy Well'.

withy: willow. *It was upling scorn and downling scorn*: ? up with his ball and down with his ball. *jerdins*: ? jordans, pitchers; other versions have 'three rich young lords'.

153. *Dives and Lazarus.* Child 56. (Eighteenth century broadsides).

Dates from the sixteenth century or earlier.

156. *John Barleycorn.* S. Baring-Gould and H. F. Sheppard, *Songs and Ballads of the West*, 1889–91

Widespread in England, Ireland and Scotland; there is a famous version written by Robert Burns. An allegory of the death and resurrection of the Corn-spirit; but it is not clear whether it really has its origins in folk religion.

161. *A Ballade of the Scottyshe Kynge.* British Museum, c.39.e.1; ed. John Ashton, London 1882

Written and published soon after the Battle of Flodden 1513.

gelawaye: Galloway. *armeleche*: Amalek. *copholde*: copyhold. *naverne*: Navarre.

163. *Whipping Cheare. A Pepysian Garland*, ed. Hyder E. Rollins. Cambridge U.P. 1922

The first part of an Elizabethan broadside.

spittle: Hospital. The sisters are prostitutes.

165. *The Journey into France.* Taverham MS. *c.* 1600–40, in the

Nottingham University Library. Ed. V. de Sola Pinto and
A. E. Rodway, in *The Common Muse*
Dated about 1623.

170. *A Ballade upon a Wedding.* Sir John Suckling's *Fragmenta Aurea*, 1646

175. *A Proper New Ballad, intituled The Fairies Farewell. Certain Elegant Poems*, 1647 by Richard, Bishop Corbet (1582–1635)

Fairies were believed to reward good housewives and punish sluts.
register: registrar. *con*: grant. *Chourne*: servant to Dr Hutten,
Corbet's father-in-law.

177. *On the Lord Mayor and Court of Aldermen. Poems on Affairs of State*, 1697; by Andrew Marvell

180. *The Dutchess of Monmouth's Lamentation. Roxburgh Ballads*, vol. V, 3, 640. 1885

Dated about 1684.

182. *Clever Tom Clinch going to be hanged.* Poems of Jonathan Swift, ed. Harold Williams; Oxford, Clarendon Press 1927

183. *Newgate's Garland. The Poetical Works of John Gay*, ed. G. C. Faber; O.U.P.

When Blake was on trial he made a murderous attack on the arch-criminal, Jonathan Wild, who was giving evidence against him. Wild recovered, to hang a few years later. This ballad is one of the germs of *The Beggar's Opera.*

185. *The Fine Old English Gentleman. The Poems and Verse of Charles Dickens*, ed. F. G. Kitton, 1903

187. *A New Song for the Birth of the Prince of Wales. Modern Street Ballads*, ed. John Ashton; Chatto & Windus, 1888

188. *Life of the Mannings. Modern Street Ballads*, ed. John Ashton; Chatto & Windus, 1888

191. *Wednesbury Cocking. English and Scottish Ballads*, ed. Robert Graves; Heinemann, 1957

The most famous of English provincial ballads.

Wednesbury (Staffs) is pronounced 'Wedgebury' or 'Wensbury'.

194. *Miss Bailey's Ghost. Modern Street Ballads*, ed. John
Ashton; Chatto & Windus, 1888

195. *Danny Deever. Barrack Room Ballads* by Rudyard Kipling. Reprinted by permission of Mrs George Bambridge,
Messrs Methuen & Co and the Macmillan Co of Canada

199. *Brian O Linn. Irish Street Ballads*, ed. Colm O Lochlainn,
Dublin 1939
Late eighteenth century, but derived from a much older
Scottish song or nursery-rhyme 'Tam O'Lin.'

200. *The Bonny Bunch of Roses. Irish Street Ballads*, ed. O
Lochlainn
Dates from the Napoleonic Wars.

202. *Dunlavin Green. Irish Street Ballads*, ed. O Lochlainn
Written soon after the events of 1798, when the English
government arrested many of the leaders of the United
Irishmen. Captain Saunders of the Saunders-Grove corps in
Wicklow arrested about twenty of his men who confessed to
having taken the oath of the United Irishmen; they were shot
at Dunlavin.

203. *The Croppy Boy. The Golden Treasury of Irish Verse*, ed.
Lennox Robinson, 1925
Also from the 1798: 'Lord Cornwall' is Lord Cornwallis, Lord
Lieutenant.
'Croppy' is a common term for the rebels of '98, who cut their
hair short in sympathy with the French Revolution.

204. *Brennan on the Moor. Traditional Tunes*, ed. Frank Kid-
son, Oxford 1891
Willie Brennan, the famous highwayman, operated in the
Kilworth Mountains, County Cork. He was a Robin Hood
figure and was hanged in 1804.

206. *Young Molly Bán. Irish Street Ballads*, ed. O Lochlainn

NOTES

Also known in England and America as 'The Shooting of his Dear'. Probably eighteenth century in origin.

207. *The Rocky Road to Dublin. Irish Street Ballads*, ed. O Lochlainn

Commemorates the Irish immigration to England in the nineteenth century.

208. *The Night before Larry was Stretched. Musa Pedestris*, ed. John S. Farmer 1896, who dates it *c.* 1816
numbing chit: gallows.

211. *Mrs. McGrath. Irish Street Ballads*, ed. O Lochlainn

212. *Johnny, I hardly knew ye. The Golden Treasury of Irish Verse*, ed. Lennox Robinson, 1925
Late eighteenth or early nineteenth century.

215. *A ballad of Master McGrath. Irish Street Ballads*, ed. O Lochlainn

Sung to the tune of 'Villikens and his Dinah'. The actual event is the winning of the Waterloo Cup by the Irish greyhound Master McGrath, in 1868, 1869 and 1871; also commemorated by a public monument.

216. *The Old Orange Flute. Irish Street Ballads*, ed. O Lochlainn
Also sung to the tune of 'Villikens and his Dinah'.

218. *Kevin Barry. Irish Street Ballads*, ed. O Lochlainn
This song is said to have been so popular in the British Army during the Troubles that it had to be banned.

219. *Finnegan's Wake. Irish Street Ballads*, ed. O Lochlainn
Mid-nineteenth century music-hall ballad.
Thanam o'n dhoul: your soul to the devil.

220. *The Ballad of Persse O'Reilly. Finnegans Wake* by James Joyce, Faber & Faber, 1939
See *Song in the Works of James Joyce*, Mabel Worthington and M. J. C. Hodgart, Temple University Press, Philadelphia 1959.

224. *Van Diemen's Land. Irish Street Ballads*, ed. O Lochlainn
Van Diemen's Land is Tasmania. Known widely in England;
a Nottingham version is given in *The Common Muse*. Before
1853, when transportation to Tasmania was abolished.

229. *The Wild Colonial Boy. Old Bush Songs*, ed. Stewart and
Keesing
Apart from this ballad, which is in the Irish tradition, little is
known of Jack Doolan; his date was probably the first half of
the nineteenth century. This is less 'literary' than the next
four, which are more typical of Australian popular verse.

230. *The Death of Morgan. Australian Bush Ballads*, ed.
Stewart and Keesing

231. *The Banks of the Condamine. Old Bush Songs*, ed. Stewart
and Keesing

232. *The New-Chum's First Trip. Old Bush Songs*, ed. Stewart
and Keesing

234. *Stir the Wallaby Stew. Old Bush Songs*, ed. Stewart and
Keesing

235. *Barbara Allen. English Folksongs from the Southern
Appalachians*, ed. Campbell and Sharp
Although a genuine Child ballad (nr. 84), from the seventeenth
century, this can be considered American by adoption, since it
became so widely sung everywhere in the U.S.A. and was a
favourite of cowboys.

237. *The Wild Rippling Water*. J. A. and Alan Lomax, *Cowboy
Songs and other Frontier Ballads*

239. *Sweet Betsy from Pike*. Lomax, *Cowboy Songs*
From the Gold Rush era.

240. *The Jam on Gerry's Rock*. Franz Rickaby, *Ballads and
Songs of the Shanty-Boy.*
A favourite lumbermen's song, probably originating in Maine
during the Civil War.

NOTES

242. *The Dying Cowboy.* Lomax, *Cowboy Songs*

Also known as 'The Cowboy's Lament' and 'The Streets of Laredo'. Based on an Irish song 'The Unfortunate Rake' of the late eighteenth century, it reached America through mid-nineteenth century English broadsides. It also gave rise to 'The Bad Girl's Lament' and the Negro 'Saint James Infirmary Blues.'

243. *John Henry.* Lomax, *American Ballads and Folksongs*

The classic American Negro ballad. The real John Henry seems to have been a Negro 'steel-driver' who worked and died in the Big Bend Tunnel of the Chesapeake and Ohio Railway.

246. *John Hardy. The Frank C. Brown Collection of North Carolina Folklore.*

This ballad has become confused in tradition with 'John Henry', but the real Hardy was a miner who was hanged for murder in 1894.

247. *Blow the Candle Out.* Lomax, *American Ballads and Folksongs.*

A folk-song of Southern English origin.

Bibliographical Acknowledgements

Child, F. J. Child, *The English and Scottish Popular Ballads.* 5 vols. Boston, 1882–98.

—, — (Student's Cambridge Edition) London: George Harrap & Co.

The Viking Book of Folk Ballads of the English-Speaking World, edited by Albert B. Friedman. The Viking Press, New York, 1956.

The Common Muse. An anthology of popular British ballad poetry XVth–XXth century. Edited by Vivian de Sola Pinto and Allan Edwin Rodway, London, Chatto and Windus, 1957.

Irish Street Ballads collected and annotated by Colm O Lochlainn. Printed and published at the Sign of The Three Candles, Dublin, Ireland 1939, 1952.

Kipling, R., *Barrack Room Ballads.* London, Methuen & Co.

Lomax, J. A. and Alan, *Cowboy Songs and other Frontier Ballads.* New York, Macmillan Co., 1910, 1938.

—— *American Ballads and Folksongs*, New York, Macmillan Co.

Douglas Stewart and Nancy Keesing, *Old Bush Songs*, Sydney, Angus and Robertson, 1957.

—— *Australian Bush Ballads*, Sydney, Angus and Robertson, 1955.

Rickaby, Franz, *Ballads and Songs of the Shanty-Boy*, Cambridge Mass, Harvard University Press, 1926.

The Frank C. Brown Collection of North Carolina Folklore, Durham, North Carolina, 1952.

English County Folksongs, London, Novello & Co.

BIBLIOGRAPHICAL ACKNOWLEDGEMENTS

English Folk Songs from the Southern Appalachians, collected by Cecil J. Sharp and Olive Dame Campbell, ed. Maud Karpeles. Oxford University Press, 1932.

Journal of the Folk Song Society, London, 1899–1931.

The Golden Treasury of Irish Verse, ed. Lennox Robinson, 1925.

Modern Street Ballads, ed. John Ashton, Chatto and Windus, 1888.

English and Scottish Ballads, ed. Robert Graves, Heinemann, 1957.

A Pepysian Garland, ed. Hyder E. Rollins, Cambridge University Press, 1932.

Index of First Lines

INDEX OF FIRST LINES